LAST ONE STANDING

*Surviving the Death and Loss of My Sibling,
Coping with Grief and Mourning,
and Becoming the Memory Keeper*

P. J. JOHNSON

Copyright © 2025 by P.J. Johnson.

All Rights Reserved. The content contained within this book may not be reproduced, duplicated, or transmitted without direct written permission from the author or the publisher.

Please note that the information contained within this document is for educational and entertainment purposes only. All efforts have been made to present accurate, up-to-date, reliable, and complete information. No warranties of any kind are declared or implied. Readers acknowledge that the author is not engaged in the rendering of legal, financial, medical, or professional advice. The content within this book has been derived from various sources. Please consult a licensed professional before attempting any techniques outlined in this book. By reading this document, the reader agrees that under no circumstances is the author responsible for any losses, direct or indirect, that are incurred as a result of the use of the information contained within this book, including, but not limited to, errors, omissions, or inaccuracies.

Printed in the United States of America

First Printing, October 20, 2025

ISBN: (979-8-9997304-2-8)

To

Janyra

Painting the Heavens
With Peace and Love.

I'll see you there.

CONTENTS

PREFACE: ALONE, BUT NOT WITHOUT STORY 1

INTRODUCTION: WHY THIS BOOK, WHY NOW 3

PART I: WHERE THE ROAD BEGINS 9

PART IA: MY STORY 10

Chapter 1: The Weight Of Loss 11
    The Day the Silence Set In 11
    The Shape of a Different Kind of Grief 14
    Things You Wanted to Say (But Now Can't) 18
    Preparing to Let Go 19
    What Remains 21
    Living With the Silence 24
    The Stillness Between Steps 25

PART IB: THROUGH LOSS, GRIEF, AND MOURNING 27

Chapter 2: When The Loss Comes 29
    Anticipatory loss 30
    Sudden Loss 31
    Ambiguous Loss 32

Chapter 3: Facing The Grief 35
    What Is Grief? 35
    What Grief Isn't 36
    What Does Grief Feel Like? 36
    How Does Grief Show Up in the Body? 37
    What Triggers Grief? 38
    How Long Does It Last? 38

Is This Normal? 39
Is It the Same for Everyone? 39
How Does Grief Change You? 40

Chapter 4: Finding The Road Forward **43**
Continuing the Walk 43
Letting Life Back In 45
Saying Yes to Now 46
Looking Forward, Not Just Back 48

Chapter 5: The Memory Keeper **51**
The Last One Who Remembers 51
Inheriting the Stories 53
Carrying It Forward: The Sacred Role of the Storyteller 54
Who Tells It Now? 56
The Weight and the Gift 56

Chapter 6: The Person Still Standing **59**

PART IC: YOUR STORY **63**
Now Tell Your Story 64

PART II: THE ROAD AHEAD **67**

Chapter 7: Tending Inward **69**
Restoring the Self 69
Caring for Yourself 70
    A. Create a Routine 71
    B. Nourish Your Body (Your Needs vs Your Wants) 72
    C. Move and Rest: Listen to What Your Body Needs 74
    D. Find Time for Your Emotional Balance 76
Mourning: Waking Up to Life 78
Remembering 80
New Ways to Remember 81

Making Room for Joy 83
Creating Rituals for Healing 84
Creating Your Legacy 86

Chapter 8: Reaching Outward 89
Reconnecting 89
Talking to the Ones Who Aren't Here 90
Letting Go of What You Can't Know 91
More than Just Things: Sorting and Deciding 92
Connecting Across Generations 93
Final Reflection – Standing on The Road Ahead 95

PART III: THE TOOLKIT FOR MOVING FORWARD 97

Chapter 9: Finding Help 99
Sometimes the first "helper" is yourself 100
   A. General Types of Help to Consider: 101
   B. Specific Resources: 102

Chapter 10: Finding Balance 105
Honoring What Was, While Living What Is 105
   Say Their Name 105
   Create a Quiet Ritual 106
   Set Boundaries Around Memories 107
   Make Space for the Present 107

Chapter 11: Finding New Connections 111
   1. Start Where You Are 111
   2. Explore New Circles 112
   3. Share What You're Comfortable Sharing 112
   4. Stay Open to Unexpected Bonds 112
   You Still Belong 112
Six Ways to Step Back into Community 113

Chapter 12: Finding Comfort In Being Prepared 115
    Start with the Essentials 115
    Where to Keep It 116
    What Do You Want People to Know? 117
    Have That Conversation 118

Chapter 13: Finding Ways To Prepare For The Next Memory Keeper 119
    Preparing the Ground 120
        A. Organize What You Can Gather 120
        B. Write Down What Only You Know 121
    Making It Easy to Find 121

Chapter 14: Conclusion 123
    Finding Joy Without Guilt 123
    Still Walking…Forward 124

ACKNOWLEDGEMENTS 126

APPENDIX 129

BIBLIOGRAPHY 133

ABOUT THE AUTHOR 137

YOUR FEEDBACK MATTERS! 139

MY GIFT TO YOU 140

- Preface -

Alone, But Not Without Story

Recently, my sister died, and with her went the only person who remembered *everything* the way I do. We were just ten months apart in age, raised more like twins than siblings. For two months each year, we were the same age—and that always confused people who asked our ages and heard we weren't twins. As young children, we were dressed alike, like twins. We shared a bedroom, childhood games, adventures, secrets, and family jokes. We knew and could recall the sweet smells coming from Grandma's kitchen, trying to catch chickens running through the yard on our great-grandparents' farm, picking tomatoes off the vine in our neighbor's yard, watching our cat give birth in our younger sister's bed, and the way Mom used to react when she caught my sister drawing on the walls. As adults, we celebrated the most special family days, birthdays, and holidays together. Off and on, depending on what was happening in her life, she lived with me and my family. She was also my travel buddy and loved helping me fulfill my bucket list. Together we saw the pyramids of Giza, climbed the Great Wall of China, and visited the home of the Dalai Lama in Tibet. The only place I could not get her to go was on a safari in Africa. She was afraid of wild animals. We shared many fond memories, both as children and as adults. Now, I'm the last one left. The last one who remembers.

Even though I have a loving husband and two grown children, I've never felt this kind of aloneness. It's not just the grief—it's something deeper. It's the silence that follows you when there's no one left who knows the stories the way you do. No one to say, "Yes, I remember that too."

As you're reading this, maybe you know what I mean, how I feel. Maybe you've lost your last parent, your only or last sibling, or that final person who held a piece of your shared past. Or perhaps you're watching someone you love carry that weight, and you're trying to understand what it's like.

This book is for all of us who have suffered loss and have now become the memory keepers. It's for those who carry the stories, the laughter, and even the heartaches of those who came before. It's about the grief of loss and, especially, the grief of being the last one standing. It's also about the quiet strength in holding onto a legacy that now only you can tell. And it's about what we do next: how we carry that loss, that history, that burden, how we share it, and, most importantly, how we keep going, even when our roots feel like they've been pulled from the ground.

You are not alone—not in your grief, not in your remembering. This is our space, our story, our community, and our road to travel.

- Introduction -
Why This Book, Why Now

This book began with a truth I could no longer ignore: I was in deep emotional pain, and I felt lost, especially when I realized that I was the last one left. Not just the last one at our family table, but the last one who remembered the stories from my childhood and of my forefathers. The last one who held the photos and knew of our long-gone ancestors. The last one who knew what each silence from their loss meant. The last. If you're reading this, you might know that feeling too.

Last One Standing is a book about what comes next when all the people who knew you best are gone. It's part of my reflection and part of an open hand, held out to you. I wrote it to tell my grief story, to lessen my pain just a wee bit. I wrote it to name the feelings that don't always have words, and to give shape to the journey of surviving not just the loss of one dear person, but of being the last thread in a once-full and colorful tapestry called family.

Before we proceed, I want to make this clear: I am not a professional counselor or therapist. I'm not here to give you advice or tell you what you *should* do. I can only share what I've learned through my own experience, in the hope that it might offer something useful or familiar to you in your own journey.

==================================

PLEASE NOTE: This book is not meant to replace professional mental health care. If you feel that you are struggling with your loss, or you feel your grief is extreme and affecting your functioning, or you have thoughts that you could hurt yourself, please seek immediate professional help.

================================

This book is divided into three parts:

- **Part I** begins with my story. It's personal and sometimes emotional, sometimes funny, but always real. We each have our own grief story. I share mine in case it helps you feel less alone in your own grief. Then you may reflect on yours.
- **Part II** explores the emotional terrain of loss—grief, mourning, memory, identity, and what it means to be the one left behind.
- **Part III** offers some practical tools, thoughtful questions, and gentle suggestions for how to move forward—not "move on," but forward—with meaning and intention.

You don't have to read the book straight through. You can skip around, pause, and come back later. Some chapters may resonate with you immediately, evoking memories and emotions. Others might not fit just yet—and that's okay.

It might be helpful to keep a notepad or journal nearby as you read. When you come across a reflection or a "Try This" section, you might want to jot something down—a response, a memory, a question, a feeling. You don't have to write a lot. Just what's on your mind or in your heart. And if you don't feel like writing in that moment, that's okay too. You can always return later and write something after you have had time to think, when your thoughts or feelings formulate into words. Or, you don't have to write anything at all. Journaling is for you, to help you express what you're going through and how it affects you.

I didn't start journaling when I began my journey through my heavy grief. At first, I couldn't. I wasn't ready to let my feelings out, even to myself. But in time, I reached a point where I needed to write down what I was thinking and feeling. Getting it out on paper helped—not all at once, but eventually. And later, looking back at what I had written gave me perspective. It showed me where I had been, how far I had come, and reminded me that I was moving forward.

That experience is why I created a separate companion journal to use alongside this book. It's designed as a guided tool to help you process your loss and navigate your journey at your own pace. Inside, you'll find carefully prepared prompts and exercises that connect to the chapter topics. These gentle prompts are meant to help guide you through your emotions and grief. Whether you write a lot or a little, daily or only when you feel ready, the choice is yours. The journal provides a private space for you to write when your heart or mind calls for it, and to reflect on where you are in your journey. It will be there whenever you need it—and you don't have to begin using it right away or when you start this book. So take your time. Use the companion journal, or your own journal, when you feel ready to release what you've been holding inside.

However you have come to this book, and wherever you are on your path, I'm glad you're here. I hope my words can help you as you travel on your journey.

Know you are not the only one.

And you are not walking this road alone.

"Unable are the Loved to die"
by Emily Dickinson

Unable are the Loved to die
For Love is Immortality,
Nay, it is Deity
Unable they that Love—to die
For Love reforms Vitality
Into Divinity.

Notice of Free Gift

I created a companion workbook to this book. It includes all the prompts and exercises in this book, plus extra space for your journaling. If you would like a copy, you'll find details on how to receive your gift copy at the end of this book.

PART I
Where the Road Begins

None of us chooses to start on this journey. But when loss happens, everything changes in an instant, and we are set upon this road. By now, like me, you have probably taken your first steps and are beginning to see how stormy your path forward can feel. I am learning how to travel mine. Alongside my story, there is yours too, because no two journeys are ever the same.

PART IA

My Story

- Chapter 1 -

The Weight of Loss

Before the healing, before the rebuilding, there is the breaking.
This is where the road begins.

The Day the Silence Set In

Burying a younger sibling is something I hope no one ever has to do. When my sister "J" died, it wasn't just the loss of a dear loved one—it was the loss of the other half of me.

We had other siblings—originally, there were four of us. We were the pickle-in-the-middle of an older brother and a much younger sister. But both of them had passed away long before our mother did. By the time we buried Mom, five years before my sister's death, it was just the two of us left. But honestly, it had always felt like that to us. Raised only ten months apart, we were more like twins than sisters. We grew up side by side, finished each other's thoughts, and held all the same memories. Since I was older, I looked out for her. She always came to me when she needed help. She was happy-go-lightly, while I was the serious one. She drew on walls. I withdrew into books. We were two parts of the same whole.

When my sister became sick, I knew the loss was coming. I thought I was preparing myself for it. But nothing prepared me for the silence that followed.

The day she died, I found myself sitting in my sister's home, alone, surrounded by her things. I felt lost, scared. I wasn't ready to let her go—not yet. I wanted—needed—to hold on to something, anything to keep her close. I slept in her bed that night, wrapping myself in her soft scent left on her sheets, hoping for happy dreams. For a few hours, I let myself pretend she was still close.

But morning came.

I got up and walked through her space—past her photos, her artwork, her elaborate furniture, her dresser covered with little jewelry boxes, the clothes still hanging in her closets, and her hairbrush on her bathroom sink. Everything was there… except her. And for the first time in my life, I felt I was truly alone. Not physically—my husband, my children, and my dear friend would be with me, loving and supportive. But emotionally, spiritually, in memory, I was now the last one standing. The only one left who remembered the way our mother fussed and tried to clean up while our father, the chef, was cooking, or how our grandmother would sit in the corner at the kitchen table, glasses on the end of her nose, as she read her Bible over her morning cup of coffee, or how we used to whisper and giggle in the dark after bedtime. The only one who knew what it meant to grow up in *our* family.

There were things to do—plans to make, people to call, text, and arrangements to settle. I had to be that big sister one last time. I had to keep it together. I had to stem the tears so I could function. But behind every phone call, every text message sent, and every checklist was a wave of grief that threatened to pull me under.

But there was one last act I had to perform first. The day after my sister died, I went to the funeral home to say goodbye to her body one final time before the cremation. I placed a small crystal angel in her cold hand to accompany her on her journey and asked for a lock of her hair. I looked at her face, etched it into my brain, then turned my back to walk away from my other half, leaving a big part of me in that cold space. Afterwards, a dear friend, who had driven over an hour to be with me, met me outside. We walked together through a quiet park. We talked about my sister. Then we took a drive to the beach—a place my sister and I had always loved. We walked, we sat, and watched the waves, and we ended the day watching the sun go down with a drink in hand. My friend didn't offer advice. She didn't try to fix anything. She didn't offer condolences. She just knew what I needed most that day: not to be alone.

This was the day the silence set in. And nothing has been the same since.

> *"I don't know why God always takes the good ones first*
> *And man, I've tried to be strong and carry on,*
> *But damn, this hurts".*
> Will Dempsey, Lyrics from *"Beat You There"*

=================================

Reflection:

If you've ever lost someone who helped define the rhythm of your life, then you may know what I mean by that kind of silence—not just the absence of sound, but the absence of *them*. Their voice, their laughter, their snoring, their footsteps in the next room, their calling your name. Sometimes it's not until the noise is gone that you realize just how much of your life was built around it.

What did your silence sound like?

Where were you when it first settled in?

When did you realize the silence?

That kind of silence doesn't go away. It becomes something you learn to live with—like a shadow that follows you, quietly, wherever you go.

The Shape of a Different Kind of Grief

God knows, I've lost people before. I've grieved before. But this grief—the grief of being the only one left—feels different. It doesn't just ache. It echoes.

My First Loss

My father died three months after I graduated from high school. I was seventeen. It was sudden and unexpected—one of those moments that changes everything in an instant. My parents were long separated, and Dad lived on the other side of the country. We had spent the prior summer with him, planning the future. Now it would not be. I didn't go to his funeral; none of us did. No one really talked about his death, our loss, or how we should process our grief. Life just went on. To this day, I'm not sure whether that made it harder or easier, only that it left a hollow space in me where something should have been—some kind of closure, maybe.

Later, in college, after I had chosen psychology as my major, I signed up for a course on death and dying. It wasn't random. I was still trying to understand what had happened, my feelings, and what I was supposed to do with all the unanswered questions I still carried. We read Elizabeth Kübler-Ross and other books on loss, and we wrote our way through grief. One assignment was to write our own eulogy—I died peacefully at an old age, survived by generations. Another way to express our feelings was to write a poem to someone we had lost. I chose to write to my father.

In that poem, I asked him the questions I never got to ask in life: Why did you have to die so soon? Why won't you be here to walk me down the aisle? Why won't you be here to teach my children how to swim?

It was the first time I had to deal with death up close. The first time I felt the kind of loss that just sits with you, unanswered. That class didn't take the pain away, but it helped me give shape to something I hadn't had words for yet. Years after his death, I was still hurting. I still had questions. And even now, all these years later, I still do.

Grief, This Time Shared

Many years later, our mother passed suddenly. I had taken her to the E.R. the night before because she was complaining of pain. They decided to keep her overnight to monitor her. I kissed her goodnight around midnight and told her I would be back in the morning. Around 6 a.m. I received a phone call telling me to come as soon as I could; she was failing. I arrived to find them doing compressions, but she was gone. I just sat there in that hospital room, staring and wondering. It was a shock. I called my sister. I mourned Mom deeply. We all did. But my sister was still there. Together, we had been or had overseen Mom's caregivers for almost five years. We leaned on each other through the loss and the pain, just like we always had. We planned the funeral together, went through Mom's belongings together, and talked about her together. As we went through her possessions, we remembered what Mom was like. We said things like, "Remember when she was shopping for that white hat to match her outfit?" and "She couldn't walk past a jewelry shop displaying sparkly jewelry" and "How picky she was about little things" and "How she loved to dance". We both smiled through our tears. We carried that loss together, and that made it bearable.

Now It's Just Me

But now there's no one left to lean on who remembers the childhood we shared. No one to say, "I know, I miss that too." The silence after my sister's death wasn't just quiet—it was empty. Grief felt lonelier than it ever had before, not because I lacked support, but because I lacked **shared memory**.

My husband and my dear friend were there for me, full of love, but they hadn't lived my childhood. They knew some stories, but they didn't know the texture of our family from the inside out. They could not know how my sister and I clung to each other when things were bad at home. They couldn't remember the bad times or the good times. They could not know what it felt like to grow up in our house, with our parents, our siblings, during our time.

And what surprised me most was the guilt. Guilt for being the one who's still here. Guilt for forgetting little details I swore I'd always remember. Guilt for sometimes wanting to set it all down—to walk away from the memories, the responsibility, the weight of remembering alone.

There's no rulebook for this kind of grief. People expect you to move forward because "You're strong", and "You've been through this before." But this time, my strength is not enough because no one beside me has lost the same person in the same way, from the same place. There's no one for me to hold on to who can say, "I know."

It's a different kind of grief—that hole in your gut—a quiet, lingering one. It's the kind that sneaks up in moments you don't expect—while folding laundry, or hearing a song on the radio, or reaching for the phone wanting to call someone who's no longer there.

It changes you. Not all at once, but slowly, like fog settling in. Not blinding, but cloudy and constant. You learn to live with it. But you also never stop feeling it.

Sometimes, it feels like I'm alone in a crowded room. Surrounded by people who care, but still somehow unseen in the depths of what I'm trying to hold onto. Because what I'm holding is memory—deep, shared, and now solely mine.

They say grief is love with nowhere to go—but sibling grief is something even more particular, different. It's the loss of a shared language, of old stories no one else knows, of the one who lived your childhood with you. They consider us as the "forgotten" or "invisible" mourners. Losing a sibling, as an adult or at any age, is just as significant as losing a parent or a spouse. With the death of a sister or brother, you don't just lose them—you lose a piece of yourself.

===============================

Reflection:

Not everyone talks about this kind of grief. It's often tucked away behind bigger, more obvious losses. But it leaves a mark just as big.

If you've lost a sibling, you may know what it feels like to carry now the memories that no one else shares—to be the only one left who remembers certain faces, certain smells, certain stories, certain experiences, family inside jokes from decades ago.

So, what do you do with those memories?

Who do they belong to now?

How can you preserve those precious memories?

That kind of grief doesn't just fade. It asks you, gently and persistently: *Will you be the one to remember?*

Things You Wanted to Say (But Now Can't)

It's the little things that catch me off guard.

I'll hear a story on the news, or something funny will happen here at home, or I'll hear or not hear from one of my kids, and I'll think, *I have to tell her this.* Or, it's Sunday, our regular day to catch up on the phone, and I go to pick up the phone. Then, just as quickly, I remember—I can't. That moment of forgetting and then remembering hits like a second loss. Over and over again.

There were so many things I still wanted to say. Stories we hadn't finished telling each other. Questions I meant to ask her, answers I meant to give. Family memories I was hoping she'd help me piece together. Trips we needed to plan. I thought we had more time. We always think we do. We were supposed to be the next Delaney Sisters.

There are also things I never got to thank her for. The quiet ways she showed up for me. The ways she supported my challenges. The times she forgave me when I didn't deserve it. The times she looked up to me or leaned on me, and I was glad to be the one she came to, she trusted. I wanted to tell her those things—just to be sure she knew. But now I have to carry those words in my heart, hoping and praying she somehow already did.

Growing up like twins, we said a lot to each other over the years—more than many siblings ever get to say. But even with all those conversations, I still find myself thinking of things I wish I'd told her. Words that come to me in the middle of the night, or while I'm driving in my car, or when I hear a certain opera aria, or when I see a piece of art she would love. Regrets that whisper in the quiet moments. And questions that will never have answers.

===================================

Reflection:

Maybe you have your own list, too.

Maybe you've also replayed a moment, rewound a conversation, or imagined a different ending.

If so, just know—you're not the only one.

What did you want to say?

What still lives in your heart, waiting for a chance to be heard?

Even if no one else hears it, it still matters. You can still say it now. Out loud. In a letter. In a prayer. Or even in silence. Sometimes, just naming the words is enough to soften their weight.

Preparing to Let Go

When someone is dying, there's a strange kind of double vision that sets in. You're caring for them in the present, even as you begin sorting out the pieces of the future they won't be there to see. My sister and I lived in different states by then—a plane ride apart—but when her diagnosis became real, we both knew it was time to talk about the hard things.

We had conversations that no siblings should ever have. What did she want done with her body? Who should get what? What needed to be put in writing, and how soon? She trusted me to take care of all that "business stuff", and I stepped into the role, once again, because that's what you do when it's always been just the two of you.

The one conversation we never had was *How much time do we still have together?*

I traveled back and forth between our states, coordinated her caregivers, arranged for her meals, managed her finances, and made sure her bills were paid. I arranged for the drafting of her Will, then made sure it was properly witnessed and signed in her home. I made sure she was safe and comfortable. We even went through some of her special jewelry—just the two of us—making sure it wouldn't disappear in a house now filled with strangers. It was heartbreaking, but it was sacred work. I was trying to get her life in order, trying to keep her safe, trying to make her happy, while holding on to what little time we had left together.

One day, in the middle of all the planning and decisions and the numerous hospital stays, she looked at me with the questioning eyes of a child and asked, *"Why is this happening to me?"* That look, that voice—it shattered me. All I could say was, *"I don't know."* I had asked God the same question more than once. I never got an answer either.

Moments like that don't just pass through you—they stay. They settle into your memory, your body, your dreams, your prayers. And if you've ever walked beside someone you love as they prepared to leave this life, you might have moments like that too—questions you couldn't answer, tasks you quietly carried, things you still hold close.

===================================

Reflection:

Have you lived through that kind of season?

Have you helped someone put their life in order, even as it was slipping away?

What did you hold onto—an item, a conversation, a memory, a promise?

Some things stay with us—not because we chose them, but because they chose us.

What Remains

As Executor of my sister's estate, I was responsible for paying her final bills and making sure her bequests were carried out. Thankfully, she had left her condominium—her home—to my daughter—her godchild, so I didn't have to worry about selling it. But her things—and she had lots of things--that was something else entirely.

Right after she died, I couldn't bring myself to go through her belongings. I wasn't ready. I wasn't able. And legally, I had to wait for the court to officially appoint me as Executor anyway. It took a little over a year before I returned to her state and settled into her home, ready—or at least willing—to begin that task.

From a young child, my sister had always been the creative and talented one. She was a professional singer, and a designer. But first and foremost, she had been an artist, and her home reflected that. Her paintings were everywhere—some of them very large—wall size—hanging on or leaning against walls in every room, stacked against the 3 walls in her guest bedroom, or tucked under tables, in closets, or in corners. I went through each one, photographing them, touching them, remembering when she painted or drew them, and what they represented. They were her life, her babies. It felt like she was still present in each of her canvases. Some had been bequeathed to me, and I chose a few more to keep. I shipped them back to my home, where they now hang, alive with her vision and color. Others were set aside for our nephew and her best friend. The remainder was left with my daughter. One of the things we had talked about was her artwork and my plans to, one day, make a book of her art, to preserve the wonder, beauty, talent, and the life of my other half. That is still the plan.

Like our mom, she also had a large collection of jewelry and jewelry boxes. I kept one small round red flowered box—not because of any financial value, it had none, but because it reminded me of her quirkiness. It sits on my dresser, empty. We packed up the rest of the jewelry to go to my daughter. I kept the bracelet my sister always wore. She had bought it while traveling with our mom. It's been on my wrist since that day when it came off hers.

And then there was her Christmas tree. My sister loved Christmas so much that she kept a decorated fake tree up all year long. I went through the ornaments, packed up the ones that were special to her—or had been in our family for years—and shipped them to my home. Last Christmas, we hung them on our tree.

"J" also made her own greeting cards—beautiful, hand-drawn or painted. I brought them back, too. Now, each year, I choose one or two to copy and send as our Christmas cards.

Her clothes were another story. She had too many. I chose a few of her big shirts—"J" was smaller than me, but she loved to wear oversized shirts—ones I remember as her favorites or ones she wore frequently. I wear them now and then. She also had favorite colorful scarves she would drape around her shoulders because she was always cold. I kept the two she loved most and wear them when I miss her, or want to feel close to her, or want her to share an experience with me.

She also had a huge shoe collection—rows and rows in every color and style—boots, flats, heels, sandals. She once said the reason she bought so many shoes was because she didn't have them growing up. Back then, we were poor. We each had one pair for school and one for church, and that was it. But later in life, when she could afford more, she made sure to have what she once went without. That collection wasn't just about fashion—it was a quiet celebration of how far she'd come.

And then there were her writings, her sketches, her poems. I brought those back, too.

There was one item I kept that was not made or bought by my sister—her comforter. My mother had made comforters for each of us: me, my sister, my son. I took it off my sister's bed and shipped it home, with my daughter's blessing.

The rest—the things not bequeathed, claimed, or sent—went to my daughter, her godchild, to keep or part with as she saw fit.

And when it was done, I walked out her door, locked it behind me, and didn't look back.

Some people say grief lives in memories. But sometimes, it lives in objects too—in the bracelet you wear, the card you send, the scarf you wrap around your shoulders, the comforter on your bed. The ordinary becomes sacred, not because of what it is, but because of *who it belonged to*.

===============================

Reflection:

Have you gone through a loved one's things?

Were there objects you kept that others might not understand—but you just knew you needed them?

What have you held on to?

And what, in the end, still holds on to you?

Living With the Silence

Grief doesn't have an endpoint. People talk about closure, but I've come to believe that's not real—not in the way most people mean it. What you get is *continuation*. You learn to keep going, even when the silence settles in for good.

For me, the hardest days are the holidays. My sister made such a big thing of them—Christmas, birthdays, anything worth celebrating. I'll never forget one Mother's Day when she decided to make dinner for our mother, our grandmother, and me. She brought out these fancy little dishes of shrimp cocktail and couldn't understand why the shrimp just draped over the sides. My grandmother looked at her dish and asked, "J, did you boil these?" It turned out no one had told her you had to *cook* the shrimp first—they were limp and raw. We laughed about that for years. That was her—big-hearted, sometimes hilarious, always trying to make things special.

At home, my husband and I had decorated our spare bedroom just for her visits. It's filled with pieces of her. Her artwork hangs on the walls. Photos of the two of us as children and grown-ups sit on her dresser. Caricatures of the two of us hang on a wall. Her sketchbook sits on the bookshelf waiting for her inspiration. We still call it "J's room." Sometimes I walk in, see her smiling face, and say, "Hi, J." On some days, it helps. On others, it hurts more. That's just how it is.

When I wear one of her shirts or scarves and someone compliments me on it, I can't just say "thank you." I end up telling them about her—who she was, what she loved, how she made people feel. Talking about her somehow keeps her a little more present.

Both she and our mother were born in October, on different dates. And, as fate would have it, both died on the Tuesday after Mother's Day—same day, different years. So that stretch of May is especially hard for me.

But sometimes, she shows up in my dreams. Not as a ghost, not in fear—just there, as her silly, happy, smiling self. Real. Whole. Familiar. And I always wish I could stay asleep just a little longer.

===================================

Reflection:

Grief changes form, but it doesn't disappear. It settles into routines, memories, even rooms. Maybe you've found that too. Maybe you have a trinket, or a smell, or a song that brings someone back to you—just for a moment.

What keeps them close for you?

Where do you still feel their presence?

And how do you carry their absence, quietly, through your days?

The Stillness Between Steps

If you've read this far, maybe you've walked or are walking this road too, or maybe you know that one day you will.

There's no map for being the last one left. No script for the silence, the longing, or the weight of memory. But if any of these pages have stirred something in you—if you've nodded, cried, smiled, or remembered—then please know this: you are not alone.

Grief, in all its quiet forms, connects us. And telling these stories— mine, yours, ours— of our loss helps us keep what matters close.

Let's keep traveling down this road. Let's face first our loss, and then our grief.

PART IB
Through Loss, Grief, and Mourning

Even after we've managed our first steps, this road does not get easier—it only changes. To understand what's happening to us, we need to pause, see where we are, recognize what lies ahead, and face how loss and grief will touch us so we can begin to prepare ourselves for the journey still to come.

- Chapter 2 -

When the Loss Comes

Loss doesn't always show up with a headline. Mostly it comes quietly, with a shift in routine or the sudden absence of a voice on the other end of the phone. Sometimes, it hits like a bolt—fast, jarring, and life-altering. Whether expected or sudden, visible or silent, loss leaves its mark. Before we talk about grief—what it feels like, how it behaves—we need to look closely at what's missing, at what was taken, changed, or left behind.

Because until you have named the loss, it's hard to understand the pain.

Loss comes in more than one form. It isn't always about death, and it doesn't always come all at once. Some losses build slowly, creeping in around the edges until one day something that once felt secure is just…gone. Others arrive with no warning at all, leaving shock in their wake. No matter how it happens, loss creates a space that wasn't there before.

Here are some of the kinds of loss people experience, especially when they become the last one standing:

- **Loss of a person:**

    This is probably the most visible and widely recognized kind of loss. When someone dies, there's often a funeral, an obituary, and a shared grief. But even within that shared experience, each person's loss and each person's response to that loss are unique.

- **Loss of identity or role:**

    When someone close to you dies, you may lose a role you didn't even realize defined you. Suddenly, you're no longer a sibling, a daughter, a partner in the same way. The version of yourself that existed in relation to that person disappears, too, with the loss.

- **Loss of home or tradition:**

    After a major loss, the places and routines that once felt like "home" can feel unfamiliar or may have to change. You may have to sell the family home, stop hosting holidays, or lose a daily ritual like a morning call or shared meal.

- **Loss of shared history:**

    When the last person who remembers "that story," "that trip," or "that nickname" is gone, you lose more than just company—you lose context. The shared memory disappears. That, too, is a kind of loneliness.

However, not all losses are defined by what is lost—some are shaped by *how* the loss happens. The experience of losing someone suddenly, or slowly, or in an unresolved way can deeply influence how we process what's missing—what's now loss. These kinds of losses aren't always about a specific role or a place—they're about the *nature* of the goodbye, and how it lands in our lives.

Anticipatory loss

Sometimes the loss begins long before you have to say a final goodbye. You may already feel the loss creeping in while your loved one is still physically present. Like it did with my sister. This is anticipatory loss—the sorrow that builds while you're watching a loved one fade slowly, piece by piece. It often happens during long illnesses, or in memory decline, or during hospice care.

You may feel helpless as you watch them retreat into pain, confusion, or just deteriorate. You might feel the loss of the shared future that will no longer happen—the plans that won't be fulfilled, the milestones they'll miss. And yet, you're still showing up, day after day, trying to hold on to what's left. That emotional weight is very real.

In some cases, you may start to notice changes—a voice that no longer sounds like theirs, a shared routine that quietly ends, a blankness in their eyes where connection used to be. Something important is slipping away, even while they're still physically present. You're already adjusting to the absence that will come while they're still here. The loss unfolds in real time, moment by moment.

What makes anticipatory loss especially difficult is that it's often invisible to others. From the outside, people may think everything is "okay" because your loved one is still alive. But inside, you're already carrying layers of sadness, anxiety, and pre-grief. It can be very disorienting. You might even feel guilt for feeling so much, so soon.

Anticipatory loss also brings moments of tenderness. Sometimes, it can also be a gift since you may be able to say things you never got to say before. It allows space for forgiveness, for gratitude, for being present, for hugs, and *for saying goodbye*. It's a kind of sorrow with both sharp edges and soft spots.

Sudden Loss

Sudden loss arrives like a hurricane you didn't know was coming. One moment you're living your everyday life, and the next—everything has changed. It might be a knock on your door or a phone call in the middle of the night; there's been an accident, a collapse, or a diagnosis that goes from concern to finality in the blink of an eye. Like what happened with my mother. There's no time to prepare, no gradual shift, no warning. Just a sudden line between *before* and *after* that you didn't choose and can't erase.

What makes sudden loss so difficult is its abruptness. There's often unfinished business—things left unsaid, plans made just days before, routines that still feel like they should be happening. You may still expect to hear a voice, give a hug, get a message, or see someone walk through the door. The world keeps moving, but you're left standing in the space where someone else should still be.

It's not just the absence that overwhelms—it's the speed of the change. Sudden loss shakes the foundation and brings trauma, shock, and sometimes an inability to even catch your breath. It can feel as if the floor dropped out from under you without warning, leaving you scrambling to understand what's just happened.

Even when you are surrounded by others, sudden loss can feel isolating. It often takes longer to process because your mind has to catch up to reality. While everyone is reacting, you're still trying to catch up to the fact that it happened at all.

Ambiguous Loss

Some losses aren't clear-cut. There's no final goodbye, no defining moment, no easy way to say what's been lost—or say how you feel about it. These are ambiguous losses.

- **When someone is gone, but not really gone:**

    Maybe they've disappeared from your life, but are still alive somewhere. Maybe you're estranged, or they vanished without explanation. The body is absent, but the questions linger.

- **When someone is here, but no longer fully themselves:**

    Maybe they have Alzheimer's, or are in a coma, or have another illness that takes away their memory or personality. Perhaps an addiction or mental illness has changed who they were. You see them, but they can't respond or don't recognize you, and the connection is broken. They're present, but not fully reachable.

- **When the relationship was painful or unresolved:**

    Sometimes, you lose someone who hurt you. Or it's someone you loved, but they never really showed up for you. When that person dies—or disappears—the feelings can be complicated. You're not just mourning a person; you're mourning what should have been, what never was, and what will now never be.

These kinds of loss don't have neat endings or obvious rituals. But that doesn't make them less real or less of a loss. That doesn't mean you don't grieve.

That's why naming them helps. Giving shape to your losses allows you to make sense of your response to them. It doesn't make them easier, but it does make them real—and that's the first step toward healing.

==

Try This:

Now that you have reviewed the list of different types of losses, take a moment to list a few of the losses you've experienced—big or small, recent or long ago. Don't overthink it. Just write what comes to mind. These might include people, pets, roles, places, traditions, or moments you can't get back.

> Take a moment to review what you have written.
>
> Put a star next to the ones you haven't really acknowledged or talked about.
>
> Maybe now is the time.

In Closing

Grief often gets all the attention, but the losses that come before it deserve to be seen and felt, too. Now that we've taken time to name and acknowledge what's missing, we can begin to understand how that loss moves through us and the effect it has on us. In the next chapter, we'll explore grief—what it is, what it isn't, and how it shows up in ways you might not expect.

- Chapter 3 -

Facing the Grief

"Grief changes shape, but it never ends." — Keanu Reeves

Have you ever felt something heavy settle on your chest after a loss, not quite pain, but not just sadness either? That's grief. It doesn't always show up right away, and it doesn't always look how people expect it to. But if you've lost someone close to you, especially if you're the last one standing, grief is part of your story—whether it's whispered in the background of your mind or shouted in your face.

Grief can be slippery. Just when you think you've understood it, it changes. Just when you think you're past it, it shows up again. In this chapter, we're going to face grief directly—not to fix it or explain it away, but to name it, sit with it, and maybe understand it a little better.

Let's start with the most basic—and most complicated—question.

What Is Grief?

Grief is the natural human response to losing something or someone important. Most people think of it in terms of death, but it can also come from other kinds of loss: the loss of a relationship, a role you once had, or even the imagined future that can no longer be.

Grief touches your thoughts, your emotions, your body, and even your sense of time. It can make days feel too long and nights feel endless. It can show up as tears, silence, anger, or a numbness that just won't lift. Grief is not a sign of weakness—it's a sign that love, once there, has gone.

What Grief Isn't

Grief is not a flaw or a failure. It's not something to be hidden, rushed, or "gotten over." People may say things like "Be strong" or "She would want you to move on," thinking they're being helpful, but those words often add pressure for you to perform rather than permission for you to feel.

Grief also isn't the same as depression, though they can feel similar. Depression can make you feel like nothing matters. Grief can make you feel that *one thing* matters too much. Grief doesn't follow a checklist. And those famous "stages" of grief? They're not a staircase, going in one straight, even direction—they're more like a spiral, turning you around and around.

What Does Grief Feel Like?

That's a question with more than a thousand answers—one for every person who has ever suffered grief. For some, it's sadness that never fully lifts. For others, it's irritation, restlessness, or sudden bursts of tears that seem to come out of nowhere. Grief can feel like emptiness, or like carrying a hundred-pound backpack you didn't ask for.

Sometimes it shows up physically: exhaustion, headaches, stomach trouble, a racing heart. Sometimes it's you forgetting things or feeling like you're moving through fog.

And sometimes, unexpectedly, there's laughter. That doesn't mean you've moved on. It just means you're human.

How Does Grief Show Up in the Body?

Grief doesn't just live in our heart or mind—it can show up in our body, too. Sometimes it creeps in quietly; other times, it hits you like a wave. Maybe you can't sleep, or maybe you sleep too much. Food might lose all taste, or you might find yourself eating when you're not even hungry, just trying to fill the silence. Some people lose weight without even noticing—meals pushed aside or forgotten. Others gain weight, using food for comfort in moments that feel too empty.

You may even feel restless, achy, or heavy, as if you're carrying something you can't put down. Some people might notice their heart racing or their chest tightening. Others may feel tired all the time, no matter how much they rest. Even things like headaches, stomach issues, or forgetfulness can be grief's way of getting your attention.

These changes can feel confusing or even scary, especially when you don't realize they're connected to the loss. But they are, or they can be. Grief has a way of working its way through the whole body. If you are concerned about the changes you are experiencing, you should seek professional help.

If these changes sound familiar, you're not alone, and you're not doing anything wrong. It's okay to be gentle with yourself. Listen to your body. Give it rest, water, movement, or quiet—whatever it's asking for. These are not signs of weakness. They are signs that your body, just like your heart, is trying to find its way through this loss.

What Triggers Grief?

Grief doesn't always need a big event to rise again. Sure, there are the obvious days: birthdays, anniversaries, holidays, or incidents—like breaking one of my sister's Christmas ornaments, which made me burst into tears. But then there are the quiet ambushes—a song on the radio, a scent in the air, a sound, a photograph, a certain look on someone's face that reminds you of them. You can be fine one moment and undone the next, with no warning.

Even good things can stir grief. A trip, a graduation, a wedding, a new baby—all can bring a flash of sorrow because the person you lost isn't there to share it. Grief can live right alongside joy, and that can be confusing. You might feel guilty for laughing or crying. You might feel both in the same breath.

Triggers are normal. They don't mean you're going backward. They mean you still care.

How Long Does It Last?

Here's the short answer: longer than most people expect. Sometimes forever—but not always in the same way.

Grief doesn't follow a schedule. There's no finish line. Some people feel like themselves again in a few months. Others still feel raw after years. And many people float somewhere in between—carrying it quietly, adjusting to it, learning to live around it.

Some days, grief may feel sharp and unbearable. Other days, it feels more like a dull ache in the background. Over time, it might, and probably will, soften—but that doesn't mean it disappears. It becomes a part of your story, a thread woven into who you are now.

Is This Normal?

Yes. Whatever it is you're feeling—numbness, tears, silence, rage, anger, confusion—it's normal.

There's no "right" or "wrong" way to grieve. You might be the one who keeps busy, who never cries, or the one who can't get out of bed. You might find comfort in rituals or feel nothing at all. You might feel like you're the only one grieving when everyone else seems to have moved on.

That doesn't mean something is wrong with you. It only means your grief is your own.

Experts have created models to help people understand grief, like the five stages (denial, anger, bargaining, depression, acceptance) or the dual process model, which says people bounce back and forth between grieving and trying to live their regular lives. But these are just maps, not rules.

Is It the Same for Everyone?

Not even close. Two people can lose the same person and grieve in completely different ways. One might want to talk about it every day. The other might go silent. One might seem "fine", and the other may fall apart. Yet both are grieving the same loss.

Grief is shaped by your relationship to the person you lost, your culture, your history, your coping style, and even your age. Some people were caregivers. Others were estranged. Some had time to prepare. Others had no warning at all.

Grief is deeply personal. Try not to compare yours to someone else's or judge how they're grieving, either. There's room for all of it.

How Does Grief Change You?

Grief leaves a mark. It doesn't ask permission—it just walks in and rearranges the furniture of your life. You may not even notice how much it's changed you until you look back later and realize you're not the same person you were "before."

Some people become more tender, more aware of how short life is. Others become more guarded, more careful with their hearts. And some become more angry at the unfairness, at the timing, at the silence left behind. You might find life has a new meaning or a sense of purpose. Or you might feel tired—tired of pretending, tired of trying to explain.

Grief can make you slower to trust, but quicker to love. It can bring a new depth to your empathy because now you understand a kind of pain that words can't really hold. And for many, especially those who are the last one standing—like me—grief becomes a quiet companion, not always visible, but always there.

You never get "over" a great loss. You build your life around it. You learn to carry it differently. And in time, you may find that grief is not only about endings—it's also about the ways we keep loving, remembering, and continuing, even when someone we love is no longer here.

> *"I did not know the work of mourning*
> *Is a labor in the dark*
> *We carry inside ourselves…"*
> from *Gabriel*
> By Edward Hirsch

===================================

Reflection:

If you've been experiencing grief—whether it's something you carry quietly every day or something that still catches you off guard—take a moment to honor it. No pressure to explain it. No need to fix it. Just permission to feel it.

What does your grief feel like today?

Where does it live—in your body, your thoughts, your routines?

What has it taken from you?

How has it changed you?

And what, gently, has it shown you?

There's no right way to grieve. There's only your way, and that's enough. Be kind to yourself. You've lost something precious. And you're doing the difficult, human work of living with and surviving that loss.

But you are not alone.

- Chapter 4 -

Finding the Road Forward

*Sometimes moving forward feels like a slow walk through fog—
one step at a time, not knowing what lies ahead.*

Continuing the Walk

There comes a point after loss when the world expects you to "get back to normal." Work, the errands, the kids, the polite conversations, the sun rising—they all resume around you, whether you're ready or not. And you may smile. You may even function. But inside, you're walking a very different path.

For me, after the loss of my sister, my best friend, that path wasn't about starting over—it was about continuing the walk. Carrying my grief beside me, not behind me. I wasn't looking for closure. I was just trying to move forward through the days without stumbling too much.

Some days felt mechanical—going through motions I didn't feel connected to. Some days, I just gave in and cried. Other days, I would catch myself laughing at something, and then immediately feel guilty for it. Grief has a way of doing that—whispering, *how dare you feel joy again?*

But here's what I've learned: continuing doesn't mean forgetting. It doesn't mean being "over it." It just means I kept going. I kept walking, slowly and quietly, step after step, in a world that had changed forever—but hadn't ended.

My sister made that easier in some ways. She was a truly joyful person—lighthearted, full of love and laughter, and always on the bright side of life. She believed in joy, in love, in celebrating every moment. She didn't want a funeral. She said those only made people sad. What she wanted—what she wrote down—was a Viking ceremony. She wanted her ashes placed in a boat and floated out to sea—well, it was really a very large lake in another country. So that's what we did. We traveled abroad to grant her wish and to commemorate the first anniversary of her death. The only part we couldn't honor was her wish to have a flaming arrow shot into the boat to set it ablaze. That would have broken every law on the books. But we floated her out on the water at sunset, in a little boat with flowers and candles, just as she asked. And then, the little boat tipped over. She would have loved it!

Then we followed her next instructions: go out to dinner, her treat, eat, drink champagne, dance, and be merry. She had left that in writing, too, more than once. She wanted us to be happy, to celebrate life—her life, and death. As she wrote, she had a good life, better than most, and "to be dead would not be that bad." That was who she was—always reaching for joy and love, even from beyond the veil.

So, re-entering the world after she was gone wasn't entirely sad. What made it hard was doing it without her. Without her ever-widening smile. Without her light at my side.

But still, I walked on.

Letting Life Back In

"When you are sorrowful look again in your heart,
and you shall see that in truth
you are weeping for that which has been your delight."
— Kahlil Gibran

Grief doesn't leave all at once. But neither does joy arrive all at once. It comes back slowly, sometimes quietly—like sunlight slipping in through the cracks of a partially opened Venetian blind. You don't always notice it at first.

I began to notice it in little things: finishing and enjoying a good meal. A warm feeling while taking a walk on the beach on a breezy day. Playing with a friend's grandchild. Showing one of her art pieces to a neighbor. A moment of laughter at a funny story that didn't feel wrong. And even though I was still grieving, I realized something: life was still happening. Beauty and joy were still showing up—without asking for my permission.

That was both comforting and strange. Because there's a part of grief that feels loyal to the sadness, like letting in joy means letting go of the person. But it's not a betrayal to smile again. Or to dance. Or to eat good food and enjoy it. It's not wrong to laugh, even when your heart still aches.

In fact, sometimes it's the greatest tribute you can give.

Letting life back in didn't mean I was "better." It meant I was still here. And slowly, I began to give myself permission to live like it.

Sometimes, it was as simple as walking into "J's room" that we had decorated for her visits, looking at her picture, and saying, "Hi, J," with a smile. Some days it warmed me. Other days, it still hit me hard. But it was part of the rhythm of continuing. I still do this. Nowadays, it's more warm feelings than hard.

Grief stayed, but its pull wasn't as strong. And memory, when it surfaced, didn't always sting the way it once had. Bit by bit, life began to feel like something I could step back into—not all at once, but enough to keep going.

===================================

Reflection:

What would it look like if you let a little more life in now?

Not all at once. Maybe not forever. Just for now.

Just crack the window. Let in a soft breeze.

Open a curtain. Let in a little light.

Is there something that once brought you comfort—or even joy—that you've been holding at arm's length?

Is there someplace you used to go that was fun that you've now avoided?

Are there things you would try if you weren't grieving?

You don't have to rush.

Just notice what's possible.

Saying Yes to Now

Truth be told, I never stopped living after my sister died. I didn't retreat from the world or give up on my routines. I had a family, a job, and people who relied on me. Life had to go on—and so did I. But it didn't go on unchanged.

There were things I used to enjoy that I couldn't anymore, not in the same way. Certain holidays, certain movies, certain songs, even certain meals came wrapped in memories that felt too heavy to unwrap. The hole she left in me was too big to ignore. Too specific. Too personal. No one else knew exactly what we shared, growing up side by side, with the same parents, in the same house, during the same years. No one else could speak our shorthand, remember our pain, know my thoughts, or finish my sentences the way she could.

So yes, I kept saying yes to life. But some yeses were quieter. Some were slower. And some came with tears behind the smile.

There's a loneliness that comes when the only other person who remembers your childhood the way you do, who has been a part of you for your forever, is gone. And no matter how many people love you—and I'm blessed with love—it's a kind of aloneness that can't be filled.

Still, I've learned to say yes to the now I have. I say yes to time with my family. I say yes to stories. To photos. To talking about my sister. To wearing her shirt and remembering. I say yes to joy when it comes, and I don't question it.

Not because the grief is gone, but because I carry it with me. Quietly. Always.

And then, one day, while going through her papers, I found a poem she had written—titled *Where the Father Waits to Take Us Home to the Shelter of His Care*. She had never shared it with me, but there it was, her words, like a message I was meant to find.

She wrote:

> *"Praying God will hold you close,*
> *and gently ease your sorrow,*
> *heal your heart and strengthen you*
> *for every new tomorrow."*

Even in her absence, she was still comforting me. Still reaching out with that soft, warm, loving light she always carried. Still helping me to keep walking forward.

Looking Forward, Not Just Back

There's a point in grief—not marked by a date or a ceremony—when you find yourself looking around again. Not just back. You still remember, still ache, still carry the weight, the loss. But your gaze shifts. You start to notice and care about the life that's happening right here, right now, right in front of you.

It's not about my "moving on." That phrase never felt true to me. You don't "move on" from someone you loved and lost. You move forward with them held inside you—in your habits, your phrases, your thoughts, your stories, your smile, your heart.

For me, that shift was slow and quiet. It came in soft moments: seeing a sunrise and feeling thankful, not just sad because my sister was no longer here to enjoy it. Laughing without feeling guilty. Making plans to do things she loved without thinking, *she should be here.* She should—but she's not. And still, I go.

I started to realize that looking forward didn't mean I was leaving my sister behind. It meant I was taking her with me. Her spirit. Her humor. Her joy.

The road ahead might not look like the one I once imagined, but it's still mine to walk. And now, I try to walk it with a heart that holds both sorrow and hope, because they can live in the same place. They can live inside me.

> *"If you have a sister and she dies, do you stop saying you have one? Or are you always a sister, even when the other half of the equation is gone?"*
> — Jodi Picoult, *My Sister's Keeper*

> I shall always be a sister.
>
> I shall always have a sister.
>
> I shall not leave her behind.

===================================

A Gentle Nudge

Maybe you're here because you're still trying to figure out how to keep going. Maybe you're already walking again, slowly, carefully, one step at a time. Or maybe you've been traveling this road for a while, but the silence surrounding you still surprises you.

What does your now look like?

What are you beginning to say yes to again?

And whose memory walks beside you as you go?

Wherever you are, just know: you don't have to have it all figured out.

Grief doesn't follow a schedule. And neither does healing.

If you've started to look around—not just back—you're already finding your way. If you've slept peacefully all night, gotten through the day or night without pills, alcohol, or tears, felt joy beside the ache, laughed without guilt, or made plans without apology—you've begun the walk forward. That doesn't mean you've forgotten.

It means you've remembered *how to live*.

- Chapter 5 -

The Memory Keeper

No one hands you this role. You just wake up one day and realize you're it—the one who now holds the memories. The keeper of names, faces, laughter, events, and silence. If you don't find a way to carry it, or to pass it on, it will all begin to fade.

The Last One Who Remembers

When someone you love dies, it's not just their presence you miss—it's the shared memories that vanish with them.

In the Jewish tradition, there's a saying: *"May their memory be for a blessing."* It's more than a condolence—it's a reminder that a loved one's life can continue to bless, shape, and inspire even after they're gone. It's a way of saying that memory itself can be an enduring gift, something that sustains us moving forward, not just something we look back on.

There are so many good family memories from our childhood: the way the house smelled waking up on Thanksgiving morning, and finally being old enough to not sit at the children's table for the meal. Decorating the Christmas tree together. Making snow ice cream. Easter Sunday. Sitting in the back seat of the car, eating popcorn in our pajamas at the drive-in. Watching Mom make our first communion dresses. Dad dunking us into the ocean for our first swimming lesson, ugh! Mom teaching us how to do ballroom dances in the living room.

Then there were memories—the good and the bad—that lived only between the two of us. The good ones were like shared treasures: our childhood games, our 'just us' conversations in the middle of the night, the way she teased our little sister since she was no longer the baby, or how we'd imitate Mom just to make each other laugh. While the bad ones—and we had more than our fair share—felt like shared scars. Our good memories don't land the same when I try to tell them to someone else, even someone who truly cares. They're not wrong; they just don't have the other half of the memory. It feels like opening a photo album and realizing every picture is missing someone who used to be right in the center of the frame.

I was reminded of that feeling after Mom died, when my sister and I were sorting through Mom's things. We found a couple of old photo albums. Mom had always been the family historian—the one who remembered names, dates, birthdays, connections—but definitely not the storyteller. One album told a different story. It held some photos of faces I didn't recognize. No notes. No names. No explanations. Just silent people frozen in times past. My sister and I stared at those images, wondering how they might have fitted into our world or our family. But now they were lost. I realized that entire lives, whole relationships, had quietly slipped away with Mom's passing. That moment stayed with me. It was a sad, quiet reminder of how easily history disappears if it isn't shared. And now, if I'm honest, it scares me to think I might be the last one who remembers, and that one day, even I might forget.

There's an ache in having no one left to remember things with you. No one to say, "Yes, that happened." No one to fill in the blanks. You become the archive.

And it's so hard to carry that burden alone.

Inheriting the Stories

When you're the last one standing, you don't just inherit the family keepsakes—you inherit the remembering. You become the one who holds the stories, the history, the names, the laughter. Whether or not you asked for the role, it becomes yours. Quietly. Gradually. And then one day you realize: if *I* don't remember, who will?

As I got older and my family size dwindled, that truth settled in. I didn't have my grandparents around anymore to tell me the stories about our family. My maternal grandmother, Rosie, had been the storyteller. She loved to talk about the family, especially about growing up in Louisiana with all of her siblings and my great-grandparents. When we were children, our parents would drive us down South and drop us off to spend summers on the family farm. It was hot. It was the country. And we were a captive audience for story time since there wasn't much else to do at night. Those were happy times, full of good food, love, and history. Those visits stopped by our choice when we became teenagers, but the stories didn't—not right away. They lived on in visits from or to my grandmother, or in long conversations with my aunt Katherine in California, who held the stories from my father's side of the family.

Our family was spread across the country—New York, Louisiana, Texas, California, Chicago, Alaska—and each place held a thread of our story. But as my grandparents and aunts aged or became sick, the storytelling started to fade. And I realized: if someone didn't write them down, they'd disappear.

I wanted my kids—and all the great-grands—to know who we were and where we came from, so I joined Ancestry.com and started building our family tree. At one point, we had five living generations. I researched names and birthplaces, reviewed census charts and marriage licenses, trying to fill in the blanks.

But here's the thing: **filling in the blanks doesn't give you the stories**. It gives you the history, yes—but not the personalities, the laughter, the gossip, the favorite sayings, the hard lessons.

It doesn't tell the smell of Grandma's kitchen as she cooked the fish Grandpa had caught that day, or show the secret flask disguised as binoculars that our aunt used when she took us to the baseball game, or the image of our conservative Mom in an evening gown leaning over a pool table taking a lesson from my step-father on how to hold a cue stick, or the way Grandpa put a birthday present bow in his hair, the same way my sister would do 25 years later.

It gives you the *who, when,* and *where*—but never the *why*.

Carrying It Forward: The Sacred Role of the Storyteller

"But I am also the holder of the memories…
I am the one who keeps the precious proof."
— Donna Ashworth

In many Native American cultures, storytelling is not just tradition—it is responsibility. The storyteller is not simply a narrator but a keeper. A protector. Someone chosen to carry the stories of the people forward so that the past is never truly lost.

Among the Chickasaw Nation, these individuals are known as Keepers of the Flame—a title that speaks not only to preserving memories, but also to warmth, guidance, and light. Their role is to ensure that their culture, traditions, stories, language, and the meaning behind them do not disappear with time.

That idea speaks to me now in a way it never did when I was younger, or before my sister died. I didn't set out to become the memory keeper in my family. I wasn't appointed or formally chosen. But somewhere along the road—after the laughter quieted, the storytellers passed, and the photos started to fade—I realized I had inherited more than keepsakes. I had inherited the flame.

In the Hawaiian culture, their stories are not just told—they are *lived*. The tradition of *moʻolelo*, which means "story" or "history," is how Hawaiians have preserved their genealogies, values, and ancestral knowledge for generations. These stories aren't limited to words. They are carried through *oli* (chants), *mele* (songs), and especially *hula*, their dance that embodies both movement and meaning.

In these traditions, the storyteller is not just a keeper of words, but a guardian of memory. Their role is deeply honored—connecting the past to the present, ensuring that the wisdom and identity of their people are never lost to time.

That idea resonates with me now. I may not chant or dance my stories, thankfully, but I carry them all the same. Through photos, through retelling family tales, through the items I've kept and the names I've recorded, I try to do for my family what the *kumu hula*—the hula teachers and cultural guides—do in Hawaii. I try to hold the meaning. I try to pass it on.

I've come to believe that wherever we are—Louisiana, California, or the Hawaiian Islands—every family needs someone to remember, to be the keeper of the flame. Every family needs someone to carry the *moʻolelo* forward. And so now, I try to carry it forward—not just for my children and their (hopefully) future children, but for everyone in my family who can no longer speak for themselves.

Maybe that's what memory really is: a form of sacred stewardship. A way to keep our people walking beside us, even after they're gone.

Who Tells It Now?

My children know the stories about my sister. They are fortunate since they knew her, laughed with her—loved her—and they've heard her stories firsthand. But when it comes to the stories that stretch further back—to our greats and great-greats, to life in the country, to long hot summers in Louisiana—the interest fades. Maybe it's generational. Maybe it's just timing. After all, none of it shows up on social media.

They don't seem especially eager to hear about life before cell phones, Wi-Fi, or video games. And neither of them seems particularly keen on picking up the mantle of storyteller when I'm gone. That part stings, if I'm honest.

Still, I know it's my responsibility now to tell the tales and write down the stories. To be the one who remembers. And maybe, just maybe, something I write down—or something they hear me say in passing—will one day spark a need to know more.

Because this is what I know for certain: it's up to me, right now, to keep the flames burning—**before the fire of our history burns out.**

The Weight and the Gift

There's a heaviness that comes with having to be the one to remember. Not the kind that knocks you down all at once—but the kind that settles in slowly. Like dust. Like time. When you're the one who holds the family stories, you don't just carry memories; you carry expectations, gaps, and sometimes guilt.

I worry I'll forget something important. I second-guess the details. Then I ask myself if I've done enough to preserve what matters—or if it's slipping away—or if it's already too late. It's a quiet kind of pressure, knowing I might be the last one who remembers a name, a voice, a face.

But still—there's a gift in it too.

The gift comes when I find a photo with a name I almost lost. When I visit the cemetery, and find a grave with the name and dates carved on stone. When I can fill in an empty space in our family tree. When someone asks me, "Do you remember...?" and I actually do. When a piece of jewelry or a handwritten note brings someone's memory back, if only for a moment. The remembering is heavy. But it's also holy.

And every time I choose to speak a name, to retell a story to a grand-niece, nephew, or cousin, to write something down, to text a photo—I am keeping a light burning, continuing the warmth. Even if no one notices right away.

I remember the day I found my grandmother's Bible. She was a deeply religious Christian woman, and her Bible was the only book I ever saw her carry. We were very close while she was alive, and so, when I came across it in my mother's belongings, I was already filled with a quiet kind of joy, a warm connection. But when I opened it, I was overcome. Inside, in her own handwriting, she had recorded the names and birthdates of her ten siblings, along with the names and years of birth of their parents, my great-grandparents, with whom we had spent those hot Louisiana summers as children. She had also written down the dates of death for five of her siblings and both of her parents.

That was more than a family record. That was *history*—preserved in ink, in her own hand, in the pages of the book that meant the most to her. In that moment, I didn't just feel connected to my grandmother. I felt connected to all of them.

Sometimes, the gift of remembering doesn't come in the telling—it comes in the discovering.

===================================

Reflection:

Take a moment to think about what you're carrying.

Have you been chosen as—or did you choose to be—the memory keeper?

What part of being the memory keeper feels heavy?

And what part, if any, feels like a gift?

Whose stories are tucked inside you?

Whose handwriting do you still recognize?

What objects or photos feel too precious to give away—even if no one else understands why?

Have you discovered any items that have been gifts?

You don't have to make sense of it all right now.

Just name what's there. Let it be real.

- Chapter 6 -

The Person Still Standing

*I didn't choose to be the last one left. No one does.
But here I am.*

I've stood at the graves of my mother, grandparents, and great-grandparents. I read the eulogy at my grandmother's funeral. I've buried my siblings—one by one—until I stood alone in a way I never expected. It wasn't sudden. It happened across years, decades. But this final goodbye changed everything.

And yet—I'm still here.

I carry their memories. Their voices. Their stories. I walk through rooms filled with echoes, through holidays shaped by absence, through ordinary days that suddenly still catch me off guard.

I'm not the same person I was before. Loss has shaped me, but it hasn't and won't erase me. Sometimes I have to give in, to cry, to grieve, to ache, but I won't give up. Grief still lives with me—but so do joy, strength, memory, and the will to keep going.

That's what it means to be the person still standing. You carry all of them with you, in you. You keep walking—not in spite of the loss, but because of it.

And you become the one who remembers.

Not just the moments of loss, but the fullness of lives once lived. The stories behind the photos. The laughter behind the silences. The real, human details that might otherwise disappear.

I didn't ask to become the record keeper. But now I see the gift in it. Recently, I've gone back to Ancestry.com. I'm doing more research, trying to fill in what I can—names, dates, places, histories. And whenever I can, I am adding photos. Because I want the next generations to *see* who they came from. Not just read about them. Not just guess.

My father-in-law once wrote a history of his life and made a present of a copy to each of his children. What a blessing that was—to have his story in his own words, while he was alive, to know where he came from, what he believed, and what shaped him. That thoughtful gift of knowledge, of identity, is something I've never forgotten. And now, I want to give that same kind of blessing to those who come after me and the other descendants of our family.

But the truth is, time is not on my side. With increasing age comes a decline in memory, and I feel that some of the memories I absorbed as a child are already slipping away. That scares me. Not for myself, but for the stories, for the history. If I can't get them written down, if I can't pass them on, if the younger generation doesn't listen, doesn't care, then they might vanish with me.

So, I keep writing. I keep telling. I keep remembering—while I still can.

I write the names. I keep the photos. I wear the bracelet. I tell the shrimp cocktail story and the one of her drawing on the walls in the house as a little girl. I say, "Hi, J." I smile. I ache. I live.

That's what it means to be the last person still standing. You hold what's been lost. And you pass it on—before time takes it from your hands.

As Darlene Kascak, a storyteller from the Schaghticoke Tribal Nation in Connecticut, once said, "You don't just say you want to be a storyteller. You're chosen. It's an honor. You are preserving, protecting, and passing down those stories."[1]

I have been chosen to be the last one, the storyteller.

That's what I'm trying to do.

---

[1] *"Indigenous Storytellers Work to Protect and Pass Down Tribal Knowledge to Next Generation"*, WSHU/ Connecticut News, by Maria Lynders, November 15, 2023

PART IC
Your Story

You've read mine.

Now it's your turn...

...to tell your story.

We'll wait if you like.

Now Tell Your Story

We are our stories. Not just the stories we live, but the ones we carry, and the ones we tell. They connect us to the people we've lost, to the people we love, and to who we are becoming. Your story is part of that thread.

Telling your story matters. It isn't just about remembering what happened—it's about honoring the love that made the loss you've suffered so hard in the first place. Speaking your story is an act of love. It's a way of saying, *they mattered. What we shared mattered. And I'm still carrying that.*

It's also a gift to *you*. When you give shape to your grief—whether in words, tears, or whispered memories—you start to let a little light into the places inside you that have felt shut tight. Because holding it all in is like sealing up a pressure cooker—eventually, the steam needs to be released. Grief can build up in quiet ways, and when we don't let it out, it can catch us off guard. One small thing—a smell, a song, a date on the calendar, a word—one trigger and all the grief comes rushing back. And you can't always control where you are or how you may react.

But when you tell your story, you let the pressure out, little by little. Each time you speak it, or write it, or remember it with intention, you make a little more room inside yourself. You might even find that you may feel just a wee bit lighter. Not fixed. Not finished. But just a bit lighter. And that would be something.

Telling your story doesn't mean you have to stand on a stage or publish a book. Your story doesn't need perfect words. It doesn't even have to be the whole story all at once. Not yet. It just needs *you*. It might mean writing it in a notebook or a journal, or speaking it to a friend or therapist. You can tell it to a photo or a patch of sky. You can speak it out loud to no one in particular or whisper it in a prayer. What matters is that *you* say it, *you* hear it. That *you* let it live outside of your head and your chest for a while. However you choose to tell it, what matters is that it gets out of you and into the world.

Telling your story helps keep your loved one close. It keeps their memory alive in a world that keeps moving forward. And it helps *you* move forward, too—even if it's just one step at a time.

You don't even have to share everything all at once. Just start with what's there, what comes out, and let it flow. This is your space. Your story. This is for you.

So, go find a quiet place, pull out your journal or a notebook, take a deep breath, and begin. Take your time. Say it how you need to.

What happened?

Who did you lose?

What do you miss the most?

What still hurts?

What do you want to remember?

You may not be the last one standing, but you may be the one who remembers, who carries, who continues.

And you are not alone.

==

Reflection:

Every person going through grief has a story. Getting your story out is good for you. However, if you feel you are just not ready for this openness now, even writing it for yourself, that's okay. You can take a few minutes to sit and reflect on your story for now. Then revisit this exercise whenever you feel you are up to it. It's your story and your timeline.

PART II
The Road Ahead

- Chapter 7 -

Tending Inward

*We live with the quiet ache of loss and,
for some of us, the reality of being the last one.
How do we go on from here?*

Restoring the Self

This part of the journey isn't about fixing grief—if only we could. It's about learning how to carry it. These next pages aren't prescriptions, but possibilities. Gentle offerings and suggestions for how to live with mourning, memory, love, loss, and longing—especially when you're the one left to remember.

We all have questions:

- How do I make sense of what I'm feeling?
- How do I stay steady when my emotional footing is shaky?
- How do I find calm in this storm?
- How do I take care of myself when that's the last thing on my mind?
- How do I move forward when my feet feel stuck in mud?

You may not have all these questions, or you may have different ones. You may not see all these possibilities—at least, not right now.

And you may not do all the things suggested here. You won't need to. But maybe, just maybe, if one of them helps you understand a little more clearly, breathe a little easier, sleep a little better, wouldn't that be helpful? Maybe something here may help you hold on a little tighter—or let go when you're ready.

It begins with the most important thing: **caring for yourself**.

Before you can reach outward, you have to make space to tend inward.

This section is for that part of the road.

Caring for Yourself

"Sometimes it's okay if the only thing you did today was breathe."
— Yumi Sakugawa

Grief can shape and mold you. It can sometimes feel like it's taking over everything. You can't sleep, you don't eat, and you've forgotten your daily routines and habits. Everything feels like it's in shambles. But even amid that pain, your body still needs food. Your mind still needs rest. And your life needs some kind of rhythm to bring stability—and maybe even a small sense of normalcy.

Some days, the hardest thing you'll do is get out of bed. When you're grieving, mornings can hit you like a wave, reminding you, all over again, of what's missing. The weight of that realization can pin you down before the day even starts.

Don't aim for perfection. Just aim for movement. If all you can do is sit up and put your feet on the floor, start there. Maybe you can open the blinds, let in some light. Maybe you can wrap yourself in a robe. Give yourself credit for every small victory, because in grief, nothing is small.

Once you're up, try to keep moving—but gently. Brush your teeth. Splash water on your face. Make your bed if you can. These aren't chores; they're lifelines. They remind your body—and your spirit—that you're still here.

A. Create a Routine

Grief doesn't follow a schedule, and neither do the emotional triggers that come with it. A song, a scent, an empty chair, a date on the calendar—any of these can hit you without warning and knock you off balance. That's why creating a routine can feel impossible at first. But routines aren't about controlling grief. They're about giving yourself something steady to return to *after* the wave has passed.

Creating a soft, predictable routine can help you feel a little more stable. Try waking up around the same time each day. Fix something simple to eat, even if it's just toast. If you're able, step outside for a few minutes of sunlight or fresh air. These aren't magic fixes, but they do help your body rejoin the rhythm of life, little by little.

Routines aren't about being productive. They're about surviving the day. And slowly, over time, they become signs of life returning—not the life you had before, but the life you're learning to live now.

Try This:

Start with one anchor for your day—just one.

- **Morning:** Choose something simple to begin your day. Open the curtains. Sit with a warm drink. Write one sentence in a journal. Offer a few words—aloud or silently—to whatever gives you strength. Stretch. Breathe.

- **Midday:** Plan a small break. Step outside. Eat something nourishing. Call or text someone who understands.
- **Evening:** Create a quiet wind-down habit. Light a candle. Listen to calming music. Turn off screens early.

Don't try to structure everything. Just give yourself one or two steady touchpoints in the day.

B. Nourish Your Body (Your Needs vs. Your Wants)

Grief affects eating in various ways. For some, the appetite disappears completely, and food might seem pointless. You may forget meals entirely, or nothing sounds appealing. For others, food becomes a kind of comfort or distraction—something to turn to when the silence feels too loud. There's no right or wrong response. But your body still needs balance to carry the weight of loss.

If eating feels impossible, start small. A few bites. A warm drink. Something simple and familiar. Keep a few easy, nourishing foods on hand, such as fruit, soup, toast, yogurt, and a favorite snack. If chewing feels like too much, try sipping on something warm or smooth. Think of it less as "having a meal" and more as "giving your body what it needs."

If you're able, set a soft routine: one solid meal a day, or even a consistent time for tea or toast. Invite a friend to eat with you or send a check-in text to remind each other.

If you find yourself eating constantly—especially out of boredom, anxiety, or sadness—pause and gently check in and ask yourself. Are you truly hungry, or are you trying to soothe something deeper with the ice cream and chocolate?

Turning to food for comfort is a natural response to pain, but it can only do so much. It won't take away the sadness. And over time, it may leave you feeling worse—physically drained, emotionally heavy, or even guilty. And that's not what your body or heart needs right now.

If you catch yourself reaching for food when what you really need is comfort, try offering yourself something else: a warm shower, a walk outside, a journal entry, a quiet cry, or a call to someone who understands. These won't "fix" the grief either—but they won't hurt you in the process.

Whether you're eating too little or too much, the goal is the same: to care for the body that's grieving. Nourish it with kindness. Forgive the fluctuations. This is a time for gentleness, not guilt.

Try This:

Grief affects appetite in different ways. Some days, you might forget to eat. Other days, you might find yourself reaching for food constantly—even when you're not hungry.

Here are a few small things you can try:

- **If you're not eating much:**
  - Set a timer to remind yourself to eat something small every few hours.
  - Choose soft, simple foods—soup, toast, smoothies, or a favorite childhood snack.
  - Eat with a friend or while watching something comforting, to reduce the pressure.
- **If you're eating too much for comfort:**
  - Pause and ask yourself what you really need in that moment—rest, comfort, connection?

- Try a short walk, a warm shower, or writing down how you're feeling.
- Sip something warm instead of reaching for more food—tea, broth, or cocoa.

Be kind to yourself either way. This isn't about discipline or control—it's about caring for your body with compassion, in whatever way you can.

C. Move and Rest: Listen to What Your Body Needs

Grief can settle into your body in strange ways. Some days, you might feel heavy and numb—barely able to move—like you're dragging through each day in slow motion. At other times, you may feel jittery, restless, or unable to settle down, as if you want to crawl out of your skin. Your energy levels may fluctuate without warning. That's normal.

When you feel that restlessness, gentle movement can help. Not for exercise. Not to fix anything. Just to release the built-up tension inside. Take a short walk. Stretch your arms. Roll your neck. Breathe deeply as you stand at the sink. Small movements can make a significant difference in clearing the fog, even for just a few minutes.

Just as important: When you're worn out—physically or emotionally—rest. Grief is exhausting. You may sleep too much or hardly at all. Give yourself permission to nap, to lie down in the middle of the day, to skip the things that don't matter right now. Sleep isn't avoidance—it's healing.

Grief takes a toll on your energy, so rest when you need to. You're not lazy. You're healing. And healing is work. If something brings you peace—a walk, a warm cup of tea, a quiet moment with music—make space for it.

The goal is not to push yourself. It's about paying attention to your body and listening to it. Move when you feel restless. Rest when you feel spent. Both are ways of taking care. And don't judge yourself for needing either.

Try This:

Grief shows up in the body—sometimes as heaviness, sometimes as restlessness. These small actions can help you respond with care, not pressure.

- **If you feel stuck or heavy:**
    - Sit up and stretch your arms overhead.
    - Walk to the mailbox or around the room.
    - Open a window and take five slow breaths of fresh air.
    - Sway or rock gently while seated—motion can soothe the nervous system.
- **If you feel wired or restless:**
    - Do something repetitive, like folding laundry or sweeping.
    - Take a short walk, even if it's just around the block or indoors.
    - Stretch slowly while focusing on your breath.
    - Listen to calming music while you move.
- **When you need rest:**
    - Lie down, even if you don't fall asleep—rest still matters.
    - Nap without guilt.
    - Create a soft bedtime routine: dim lights, quiet sounds, something soothing before sleep.
    - Let yourself do less. Healing is hard work.

You don't need to do all of these. Just pick one that fits how you feel in the moment. Your body is grieving too—give it what it needs.

D. Find Time for Your Emotional Balance

Grief doesn't only live in and affect your body—it takes up space in your mind and emotions, too. You may feel foggy, irritable, restless, angry, or numb. Your thoughts might race or repeat. Your emotions can swing from sadness to guilt, from rage to a kind of emotional stillness that feels like nothing—and everything all at once. This isn't weakness or failure—it's your mind trying to understand a world that has shifted.

That's why finding small moments of **calm** can help. Not to push the grief away, but to give your system a break from grief's weight. This could be as simple as stopping to take three slow breaths or watching a candle flicker. It could be sitting on a porch, listening to the wind moving through the trees. Or silently watching the sun sink below the horizon. Or sitting by the ocean, letting the waves remind you to breathe. These quiet moments can gently steady the ground beneath you.

Solitude can also be part of this balance. Sometimes, the most healing thing to do is to step away from the noise, from the people who want to be helpful, from life going on around you. Sometimes, the right thing may be to sit alone with your thoughts and process them. That may mean excusing yourself from those around you who are there to help and finding an alone spot for as long as you need it. They will understand. It might mean expressing your feelings out loud, writing them down in a notebook, or taking a moment to meditate. Alone time isn't the same as loneliness. It can be a way to hear yourself again, especially when the world feels too crowded, too loud.

When my stepfather died suddenly, my mother found herself surrounded by people wanting to help. The "condolences", the "sorry for your loss", the dishes of food, the company, were all too much for her. What she wanted was some time alone to process, some solitude.

She got into the routine of disappearing into her bathroom, sitting on the tub, and calling me on the phone to complain about the "helpful" people. Mom was very independent, and she loved to do everything herself. She would sit and think and be alone. That is what she needed.

And if you feel angry, know that you're not alone. **Anger** is a normal part of grief—it can come from pain, confusion, or feeling powerless. Let it have its space—throw something, hit something—safely. Talk it out. Write it down. Move your body. You don't have to justify it. You just have to acknowledge it.

And sometimes, grief goes deeper. It's not uncommon to experience **depression** while grieving, especially when the sadness lingers or when everything begins to feel flat, heavy, or empty. If you find yourself feeling hopeless, withdrawn, or numb for long periods of time—if you stop caring about things you used to, or feel like you're disappearing into the background of your own life—it could be something more than grief. It could be depression. That's not a sign of weakness. It's a sign that your pain needs care and support. Talk to someone. A friend. A doctor. A counselor. You don't have to carry this alone.

Emotional balance doesn't mean feeling peaceful all the time. It means dealing with unresolved feelings and honoring what you feel, without getting swept away. It means giving yourself space to fall apart and to gather yourself back together, no matter how slowly.

Try This:

- **Name what you're feeling.** Out loud or in writing. Even if it's just, "I don't know what I feel right now."
- **Let your emotions move.** Cry. Scream. Throw something (safely). Walk. Run. Write what you're feeling in a journal.

> Scribble. Paint. Allow your feelings to rise and pass without judgment.
>
> - **Take a quiet moment each day** to simply sit and breathe—no phone, no people, no task. Meditate. Pray. Take note of your breathing and surroundings.
>
> - **Find a calm space**—a porch, a bench, a park, a car, a beach—and spend some time there doing nothing but observing.
>
> - **Create a small calming ritual.** Light a candle, meditate, pray, play soft music, drink tea, or look at the sky. Let it be your moment of reset.
>
> - **Use grounding prompts:** "I am safe right now." "This feeling will pass." "I am allowed to feel what I feel."
>
> You don't need to feel better right away. These small moments of calm are simply reminders: you're still here, still breathing, and still allowed to feel every emotion as it comes.

Mourning: Waking Up to Life

Once we have taken care of our well-being needs, we can better cope with what we are going through and how we are feeling. Sometimes, grief can feel like a heavy blanket you can't shake off—something that settles into your bones and makes even the smallest things feel impossible. But mourning is different. Mourning is what happens when grief begins to move. When you start to stretch beneath that heavy blanket, even just a little. When you take one small step toward life, not because the pain is gone, but because something in you is ready to breathe again.

Mourning isn't forgetting. It isn't leaving your loved one behind. It's waking up to life with that loss alongside you.

It might first raise its head when you are back in the grocery store and not crying in the coffee aisle this time. It might sound like your laughter when you didn't expect that story to be funny, or the first time you notice a sunset again. Mourning shows up quietly, in the moments when you feel your heart turn toward the living, even when it still aches.

This part of the journey doesn't come on a schedule either. It's not a straight line. Some mornings you will feel okay. Others, you'll feel like you've gone backwards again. That's normal. Mourning is about learning to carry your grief differently, not perfectly.

And here's something important: letting yourself live again is not a betrayal. Joy, laughter, even peace—they don't erase your love or your sorrow. They just mean you're human. You're healing. You're still here.

There's no need to rush, even if you could. But when the moments come—when you find yourself smiling without guilt, or reaching out to someone, or planning something again—let them in, let that happen. That's mourning, too. It's the slow return of light.

Try This:

Take a few minutes to think about your own experience. Has anything shifted, even slightly?

- Are there moments you've felt more present, if only for a breath or a day?
- Have you laughed, even unexpectedly?
- Have you caught yourself planning something, or looking forward to something, even just a little?
- Has there been a moment when the world felt *almost* normal again?

> Write down one or two of those moments. No matter how small. Then ask yourself: *What helped that moment happen? And how did it feel?*
>
> You don't need to do anything with the answer. Just notice. Mourning is made of small steps. You may be further along than you think.

Remembering

How often do we say it?

"Remember that time...?"

"Do you remember when...?"

Sometimes we ask it with a smile, other times with tears, always hoping someone else remembers too. Because remembering isn't just about the past—it's also how we carry love forward.

Maybe it's a silly story you've told a hundred times. Or maybe it's the way they always mispronounced that word—my southern Mom used to pronounce "oil" as "earl"—or it's the funny face they made when you were trying not to laugh. These moments matter. They're small, but they hold so much weight. Now they can help us stay connected to the people we've lost—and to who we were when they were here.

Grief can often be loud. But remembering? Remembering can be quiet. It might come as a whisper when you pass a place you used to go together. Or in a laugh that sounds just like theirs. Or as a sigh when you pass a photograph of you two, way back when.

But remembering isn't about staying stuck in the past. It's about honoring it. It's about giving shape to what was once real and beautiful—and most often complicated—and keeping that part of your loved one alive in your heart and in your life.

Sometimes, remembering brings tears. Other times, it brings comfort. Most often, it brings both. And that's okay.

And remembering isn't just for your own heart. It's also a gift you give to others. When you share stories about the people you've lost, you invite others to know them too. You're building a bridge between what was and what still matters now.

So, please take time to remember. On purpose. Out loud. In writing. In silence.

New Ways to Remember

Memory doesn't always live only in our minds—it also lives in our hands, our habits, and our creativity. Sometimes, remembering takes on a new shape when we give it form.

You don't have to be a writer, photographer, or artist to keep memories alive. You just have to start. Maybe it's making a scrapbook filled with old photos and handwritten notes. Maybe it's putting together a recipe book with your mother's or sister's handwritten recipes still smudged with flour. I have one of those. And every time I pull it out, it's not just about making the apple cake or cranberry relish—it's about hearing their voices again, directing again, having them in my kitchen again. Or maybe it's an audio recording of your voice telling their stories, or a playlist of songs that remind you of them.

A dear friend of mine passed away a few years ago, leaving behind a list of his ten favorite musicians. Each year, on his birthday, his wife chooses one of those artists, and we each pick a song by that musician to play in our friend's memory. It's simple, but powerful. It connects us all to him—and to each other.

I also do something with my sister's art. She loved making greeting cards, especially around the Christmas season. After she passed away, I began turning her drawings into our family's Christmas cards. Each year, I choose one or two of her designs for the cover. On the back, I include a small picture of her waving and the words, "Made by J." It's my way of keeping her creativity alive in the world—of letting her still be a part of our celebrations.

There are no rules. You might find yourself telling the same story over and over again. Or you can light a candle on their birthday, wear their favorite color on a hard day, or frame a letter they once wrote to you. You might want to write something down, pass along a tradition, share a recipe, or look at old photos that make you smile through the ache. You can create a ritual, build a family tree, write their name in the sand, or carve it into a tree. It doesn't matter what shape it takes. What matters is that you do something that feels meaningful to *you*.

Remembering isn't just about looking back—it's about holding on in a way that lets you carry them forward. That's remembering. That's love continuing.

Let their story be part of your story. Because even though they are gone, love does not end.

Try This:

Choose one memory you want to preserve. Think of a way to give it form: write it down, draw it, tell it out loud and record yourself, or find an object that represents it. Don't worry about how it looks or sounds. It's for you. Just let it live outside your head—so you can come back to it when you need, and so someone else can find it later.

Making Room for Joy

Grief and joy are not opposites. They live side by side inside you, often in the same breath. But when you've lost someone you loved deeply, joy can feel complicated—like a betrayal, or like something you no longer deserve. It can sneak up on you and then vanish just as quickly, leaving guilt in its place.

But here's the truth: your grief is not a wall that keeps joy out. It's a door—partially open—that joy learns to enter through quietly. Sometimes it slips in unannounced—through the smell of your loved one's favorite perfume, through laughter with a child who doesn't know the whole story of what you've lost, or through music that lifts you when you didn't even know you needed lifting.

My sister and I both loved Adele. One Christmas, I gave her Adele's latest album as a gift. Last year, after she was gone, my husband surprised me with tickets to see Adele in concert. I sat in that theater thinking, *"I would be so jealous!"* and, as Adele sang, I found myself watching and enjoying the show—imagining how much she would have loved it too. That joy didn't push away my grief. It walked musically beside it.

Joy doesn't mean you're "over it." It means you're *living with it*. It means your heart still works. That you can still feel deeply. That the loss of their love didn't close you off from feeling joy—it left a window to your heart slightly ajar.

Making room for joy doesn't mean forcing happiness. It means you can notice light where it filters in. You can let yourself smile without apology. You can let yourself rest, laugh, even in grief. Especially in grief.

> **Try This:**
> Think of one thing that brings you quiet joy. A moment. A ritual. A song. A place. A food. It can, but it doesn't have to, be connected to your lost loved one. Then give yourself permission to experience it fully, without guilt, without explanation. Write down what it feels like. What it opens in you. Let it be part of your healing.

Creating Rituals for Healing

Grief is not linear. It circles back, shows up uninvited, sometimes triggered by special events, and it changes shape over time. Rituals offer something steady in the midst of all that shifting. They don't make the pain disappear, but they give it a place to go. They create moments of pause, of meaning, of remembering.

A ritual can be anything done with intention, such as lighting a candle on their birthday or playing their favorite song when you need to feel close. It could be cooking a dish they loved or visiting a place you once shared. Even writing a note and burning it or speaking their name out loud in the quiet of your day can become your ritual to deal with your grief.

Some rituals are rooted in the belief that memory itself is sacred. In Jewish tradition, loved ones are honored with acts such as lighting a *yahrzeit* candle on the anniversary of their passing or reciting special prayers during holidays. These acts are tied to the phrase: *"May their memory be for a blessing"*—from Proverbs 10:7: *"The memory of the righteous is a blessing..."* The idea is that remembering can be more than looking back—it can be a way to bring peace, presence, and meaning into the present moment.

Some of my rituals are small, but they hold great significance for me. When I walk into my sister's room, I still say, *"Hi J."* I create our family Christmas card using one or two of her drawings. It's my way of still keeping her as a part of our celebration. On their birthdays, I post photos of my mom and sister online and wish them "Happy Heavenly Birthday." It's a simple act, but it keeps their names and memories alive to me and to those who knew and loved them.

My friend's widow has a ritual of choosing one musician from his list and inviting us all to play a song by that artist on his birthday. It's a collective ritual, and we all feel closer to him for it.

Some cultures have long embraced the idea that remembering can be a celebration. *Día de los Muertos*—the Day of the Dead—is a beautiful example. Observed in Mexico and by many others around the world, it's a holiday that honors passed loved ones with altars, candles, marigolds, music, and food. Families gather, not to mourn, but to welcome the spirits of their ancestors, to laugh, to share stories, and to feel their presence in everyday life. It's not about forgetting sorrow—it's about remembering with love and joy.

Rituals can be private or shared. They can be quiet or full of laughter. They can help us mark time, honor memory, and tend to our grief. They can give us a way to carry love forward in motion and meaning. And the beautiful thing is: you can create new ones anytime.

Try This:

Choose a simple ritual you could begin this week, or when grief happens to circle back. It might be lighting a candle at the same time each day, or playing the music they loved, or setting aside a few minutes to write or speak to the person you miss. You might want to do it on a specific date, or simply when your heart needs it. Let your imagination and memories lead you. Let it be small. Let it be yours. Let it become a thread in your healing.

Creating Your Legacy

When you've spent so much time remembering others, you may forget: you're a part of the story, too.

Legacy isn't just about what people leave behind when they die—it's what we're creating right now, every day, with the lives we live, the work we do, the people we touch. Thankfully, it's not always about big accomplishments or public recognition. Sometimes it's about the little things-a recipe you passed down, a phrase you always said, the way you always hugged everyone—even strangers—your laugh, your quirky outfits, the people you've touched, and the feelings people had when they were around you.

As the last one standing, you carry so much family history. But you also carry the future. The way you show up now—how you love, what you value, and what you choose to share—*that* becomes the story someone else will hold and, hopefully, recall one day.

You may already be building your legacy without even realizing it. Maybe it's through the way you're always there for family, or the kindnesses you offer neighbors and friends. It could be through the stories you tell about the memories you preserve. Yes, and the art or wisdom or laughter you leave in your wake, those things matter too.

Even my children don't know many stories from my childhood. They know the basics. Things we take for granted about our lives—our upbringing, our decisions, our hopes, our memories—may one day be the very pieces our children or grandchildren wish they understood better. Our descendants inherit so much more than just our name, our looks, or our photos. They inherit our voice, but only if we choose to share it, and only if they choose to listen. Maybe we can't give them the whole story, but we can give them *bites of the apple*—small pieces of who we were and how we got here—to nourish their thoughts and questions long after we're gone.

Your story isn't just about what you've lost. It's also about what you've done, what you do, and what you still have to give.

> ## Try This:
> Write a short note to your future self—or to someone who might one day want to know your story. What do you hope they'll remember about you? What values do you want to pass on? What pieces of yourself do you want to leave behind? What memories do you keep, as the last one standing, that you do not want lost?

- Chapter 8 -

Reaching Outward

How do we move from turning inward to the difficult work of letting go, accepting life as it now is, reaching out toward others, and what lies ahead?

Reconnecting

When you've spent some time tending to your own heart, a quiet shift can happen. You may start to notice there's a world around you again. There's the sound of voices, the pull of memories, the ache of unfinished conversations. And maybe—just maybe—a small part of you is ready to reach outward.

This section is about that next step. It's about reconnecting with those you've lost, with those still here, and even with the future. These pages offer ways for you to communicate with those who are no longer with you. To share your stories with people who never got to know them. To find comfort in connection and meaning in memory.

Hopefully, now, we can also begin to face the objects and spaces that hold history—sorting through things, letting go of what we can, holding on to what matters most. It's not easy. But it's part of the work of grief, too.

You don't have to have all the answers, especially now. You definitely don't have to feel "ready." But if your heart is beginning to turn toward others—even with uncertainty—you're in the next stage on your journey.

This part of the road is about rebuilding connections. And remembering that you don't have to walk it alone.

Talking to the Ones Who Aren't Here

Grief doesn't always speak in full sentences. Sometimes it comes out in whispers, questions, or one-sided conversations. You may find yourself talking to someone who's no longer physically present—while doing the dishes, driving, taking a shower, or sitting quietly with a photo. You're not imagining things, and you're not going crazy. You're processing. You're remembering. You're continuing a relationship that hasn't ended—it's simply changed.

There's no "right" way to do this. Some people write letters to their loved ones. Some speak out loud, talk to photographs, converse in the shower, or in front of the mirror. While others carry the conversation silently in their heads or hearts. These moments can be healing. They can offer a chance for you to say what was left unsaid, to seek comfort, or even just to feel close again.

Don't worry about what others might think. You don't need permission to talk to someone you love. Whether it's a whisper to the wind, a line in a journal, or a smile toward a favorite photograph, these connections are yours to keep.

Try This:

Write a letter to the person you miss. Start with something simple, like "I've been thinking about you." Or, "I wish you could see…" Let the words come as they may—no need to make them perfect. If it should get a little tear-stained, that's okay. This letter is for you.

Letting Go of What You Can't Know

There are always questions left behind. Always blank spaces that we will never be able to fill in.

What actually happened on that one vacation trip home? Why did they make that decision? What was she thinking when she wrote that letter? Who are those people in the old photographs with no names? We are left with gaps in the story—missing pages we'll never be able to find.

It's human to want to fill in those blanks. We search through boxes, scroll through records, replay old conversations in our heads, hoping something will click. But sometimes, the truth is this: we won't ever know. Not fully. Not clearly. Not the way we want to.

After Mom died, and we found that photo album with faces we didn't recognize—no names, no context, just silent images, I so wanted to fill in the missing pieces. But I can't. As I mentioned earlier, that moment was a sharp reminder of how easily entire lives can vanish when no one is left to tell the story.

And there are bigger questions, too—ones that linger in the background of a life, my life. I knew that my father's mother had died when he was very young, and that he and his baby sister were raised by their older sister, my Aunt Katherine. But I never asked my father or my aunts about my father's father. Now, they are all gone, and there is no one left to ask. And no matter how much research I've done recently, I haven't found any information that tells us who he was. His full name, his story—nothing. He's the man whose family name we carried all our lives, and my brother's children and grandchildren still carry that name. Yet he remains a mystery. That absence sits quietly in my history, and I've had to learn to live with it.

That's one of the hardest parts of being the last one left. The trail to answers has ended. And we have to find a way to live with that.

Letting go doesn't mean forgetting. It means making peace with the mystery. It means honoring the people we lost without needing their stories to be complete. It means knowing that love doesn't require full understanding. Sometimes, it's enough to say, *I don't know—but I remember. I care. I carry it anyway.*

Try This:

Write down one question you still wish you could ask. One thing you may never know. Then, underneath it, write a sentence that gives you permission to live with the unknown. It might be, *"I may never have the answer, and that's okay."* Or, *"This question matters—but it doesn't define everything."*

More than Just Things: Sorting and Deciding

At some point, the time comes to open the closets, the drawers, the boxes. To touch the things they left behind. Some of it will make you smile. Some of it will bring you to your knees.

Every item feels like a question: Do I keep this? Do I let it go? What does it mean if I do? It's never just about the object—it's about what it represents. A coffee mug becomes a morning ritual you shared. A jacket still carries their scent. A handwritten note, a favorite book, an album, a doll, a pair of shoes by the door—they all echo a life that once filled the room.

With my mom, I kept one of her hats—even though I don't wear hats. But she was known as "the hat lady" at her church. That hat was just her. I also kept and wear one of her favorite shirts. With my sister, I kept a few of her shirts, as I've shared earlier, and a small jewelry box.

I also have so much of her artwork—her sketches, her cards, her ideas. I also kept the quilt my mother had made for my sister's bed. It has two special meanings. There are things I still can't give away. At least not yet. It's still too raw. Some part of me still needs them nearby.

There's no right timeline. There's no perfect method. You can do it all at once, or a little at a time. You can do it alone or with someone who understands. What matters is honoring both *their* life and *your* healing. Some things you'll keep forever. Others, you'll photograph or write about. Some you'll pass on to others who will cherish and love them. Some you will donate, or maybe sell. And some things, even meaningful ones, you'll eventually decide to let go of—and that's okay.

Letting go doesn't mean forgetting. It means making space—sometimes for peace, sometimes for practicality, sometimes for joy. What you keep doesn't have to be what others expect. And what you release doesn't diminish the respect or the love you shared.

> **Try This:**
> Choose one object that you've been unsure about. Hold it in your hands. Think about it. Ask yourself: *Does this bring me comfort or pain? Is it something I want to carry forward—to see in my future—or is it time to say goodbye?* There's no right or wrong answer. If you let it go, consider writing a short note or journal entry about it—what it meant to you, what it reminds you of—so the memory stays, even if the item doesn't. You can hold that memory note as long as you need, or discard it if it makes you feel lighter.

Connecting Across Generations

One of the hardest parts about being the last one standing is realizing that younger family members don't remember the stories the way you do—if they even know them at all. You carry names they've never heard, jokes they've never laughed at, and lessons they haven't learned yet. At first, that can feel like a wall. But it can also be a bridge.

The stories you remember don't have to be lost. They can be passed on, not just through facts and dates, but through connection. That might look like sitting down with a grandchild and telling them what their parent was like as a kid. Or telling a nephew he has ears just like his grandfather's and then pulling out photos to show the comparison, which leads to talking about what his grandfather was like. Or maybe opening an old photo album you keep on the coffee table and explaining who everyone was and what made them special. Or writing a memory in a birthday card to your grandchild or niece. It doesn't have to be formal or perfect. It just has to be real.

Sometimes it starts small. Like when my great-nephew came to visit me with his children. Growing up, he hadn't had much connection to my side—his grandfather's side—of the family. He knew me, my sister, our brother (his grandfather), and our mother—his great-grandmother. But not much more. During that visit, I started telling them about my grandparents—his great-great-grandparents—and their life in Louisiana. Just a few stories. But it sparked something in him. He wanted to know more. Before he left, I promised to send him more stories. That one conversation began to build a bridge.

Sometimes younger generations don't know how to ask—or don't yet understand why it matters. But that doesn't mean they aren't listening or absorbing. Seeds are still being planted. You may be the only one who can link them to a past that gives meaning to their present.

And sharing isn't just for them—it's for you, too. It reminds you that the story continues, even if the cast of characters has changed.

> **Try This:**
>
> Think of one person in your family—maybe a child, niece, nephew, or grandchild. Write down or record one story you want them to know. It could be funny, meaningful, or just ordinary. Then find a way to share it: tell them in person, send a voice memo, tuck it into a card, maybe with a picture, or save it for later. The important part is you get it out of your head and into their hands.

Final Reflection – Standing on The Road Ahead

If you've made it this far, take a breath. You've carried a lot—memories, questions, silence, joy. You've looked back and then leaned forward. That's no small thing. That takes courage.

Being the last one standing can often feel like you're standing alone. But you're not. You are surrounded by echoes, by stories, by love that doesn't leave just because the people did. You've made space for the sorrow. You've honored the memories. You've spoken to the silence, and maybe, just maybe, you've started to make peace with what you'll never fully know.

You've remembered. You've sorted. You've shared. You've created. And in doing so, you've found ways to live forward—not beyond the grief, but alongside it.

This journey isn't about finding closure. It's about continuing—through meaning, through motion, through quiet acts of remembering and love. It's about how you carry what matters. How you keep stories alive, and how you begin to write your own.

You are not just what you've lost. You are what you've chosen to hold on to, and what you've decided to pass on.

Keep writing. Keep talking. Keep remembering. Keep making space—for grief, for healing, for the unexpected light.

Let that be enough. Let that be everything.

Keep going. You can do this.

PART III
The Toolkit for Moving Forward

If I could ask for one kind of support right now—without guilt or explanation—what would it be?

You may not have an immediate answer to that question, but simply asking it can begin to loosen the tight knot of grief around your heart. This next part of the book offers tools, resources, and gentle suggestions for navigating life as the one left behind. You may not need every suggestion here. Take what speaks to you. Leave the rest for another time—or never. Just know that options do exist to help you move forward, and you're not alone as you explore them.

- Chapter 9 -

Finding Help

"Asking for help does not mean you are weak; it means you are wise enough to know you don't have to carry it all alone."

Let's face it, you may be doing just fine handling your feelings and loss. Or you may be holding it together on the outside while you're quietly unraveling on the inside. Grief wears differently on everyone, and there's no single right way to heal. Some people get by with long, quiet walks alone, some by working up a sweat performing physical exercise, and others by journaling, meditation, or by conversations with family, clergy, or trusted friends. Others reach a point where talking to a counselor or joining a support group makes all the difference.

If you're wondering whether you "need" help, that alone might be a sign to check in with yourself. Are you having trouble sleeping, eating? Feeling stuck in sadness? Too many teary moments? Too many pills or drinks? Are you avoiding places, people, or conversations that remind you of your loss? Are you glued to a place or an object because you associate it with your lost one? Or are you holding in your pain because you think no one would understand—or because you think you *should* be stronger? These are just a few of the real, valid signals.

There's strength in seeking help, too, not weakness. Therapy can give you tools to make sense of your loss. Support groups remind you that you're not alone. Sometimes, faith leaders, grief books, and even podcasts can offer wisdom or language when yours runs dry. If you've been the "strong one" in your family, it might feel strange to you to ask for support, but even the strongest people need rest and care and, sometimes, someone to lean on.

Not everyone requires the same kind of help. Some want to talk; others want quiet. Some want to hear from others to realize they're not alone with their feelings. Some heal through community, and others through solitude. The point is that you should get to decide what's good for you and what works. And if what you're doing isn't working, you get to try something else.

Sometimes the first "helper" is yourself

Before you reach outward, consider starting with the first and closest source of help—you. Taking time to check in with your own thoughts and feelings can steady you for the steps ahead. For some, a gentle way to begin to help yourself heal is through writing. One simple way to do this is through journaling, giving those thoughts a safe place to rest.

You can write letters to someone you've lost, explore memories you're afraid of forgetting. Alternatively, you can create your personal grief journal and ask, "How am I doing today?" or describe the struggles you may be having being around others, or how you're feeling physically, emotionally, or spiritually today. Journaling doesn't have to be pretty or profound. It's just a place to put things you can't say out loud yet or that you don't want to share. You can scribble your anger or write about your sadness and let tears fall. You can connect with yourself.

Grief can cloud your thoughts; writing helps you untangle them. You don't need to share what you write. You can write and tear it up, or burn it, or put it away to reflect on at another time. This is for you. The act of naming your feelings—even privately—can be powerful medicine. If journaling works for you, that's great. If it's not for you or it doesn't help you, then you may want to consider a different kind of help.

A. General Types of Help to Consider:

- **Friends and Family** – Sometimes just having someone who listens, sits with you, or helps with everyday tasks can make a huge difference. It's okay to lean on people who care about you. Let them show up and be there for you, even if they're not sure how. Tell them what helps—whether it's a phone call, a walk, a meal, or just quiet company.

- **Clergy or Spiritual Advisors** – If you come from a faith tradition, clergy or a spiritual person can be a source of comfort and clarity, especially if your grief is tied to spiritual questions or a loss of meaning. Even if your relationship with religion has shifted, talking to someone grounded in ritual and reflection can offer peace, perspective, or just someone who understands sacred loss.

- **Support Groups** – These groups create a space where you can meet others who have walked a similar path. Sharing stories—or simply listening—can ease isolation and help you realize you're not alone. Hospitals, hospices, places of worship, or community centers often provide support groups. Some meet in person, others online.

- **Licensed Therapists** – Grief counselors or therapists can help you explore complicated emotions, trauma, or the long-term effects of loss. They're trained to help when things feel overwhelming, when you're stuck, or when something feels too heavy to carry alone. Many therapists specialize in grief, family loss, or trauma. You can search online or seek a referral from a doctor to find someone who fits your needs.

- **Books and Podcasts** – Sometimes reading their stories or hearing from someone who's been there can feel like a lifeline and help you realize you're not alone.

B. Specific Resources:

- **GriefShare** – griefshare.org

  A faith-based support group network offering free 13-week group sessions around the country.

- **The Dougy Center** – dougy.org

  Offers resources and support locally, nationally, and internationally for grieving children, teens, and adults, with a focus on family grief before and after death.

- **The Sibling Grief Club** – siblinggriefclub.com

  An online resource offering webinars designed to connect bereaved adult siblings, with the sole intention of lending comfort and support to one another.

- **What's Your Grief** – whatsyourgrief.com

  Promotes grief education, exploration, and expression in both practical and creative ways, with online resources featuring articles, online courses, podcasts, and printables for all kinds of grief experiences.

- **Adult Sibling Grief** – https://www.adultsiblinggrief.com

  An online resource and supportive community for adults grieving the loss of a sibling. Offers articles, a Facebook support group, and helpful tools tailored to sibling grief.

- **Therapy for Black Girls** – https://www.therapyforblack-girls.com

  An online resource with a therapist directory focused on supporting mental wellness of Black women and girls.

- **National Alliance for Children's Grief** – childrengrieve.org

  A national organization of professionals dedicated to supporting children and teens who are grieving a death, and the networks and communities surrounding them.

- **Hospice Foundation of America** – hospicefoundation.org

  Offers education and support services related to end-of-life care and bereavement.

- **Psychology Today Therapist Finder-** https://www.psychologytoday.com/us/therapists

  Search by zip code, insurance, specialty, or identity to find a licensed therapist.

- Chapter 10 -

Finding Balance

*One of the trickiest balances we may have after a loss is
holding space for our memories while making room for our lives.
The goal isn't to "move on" or "get over it".
It's to move forward while carrying what matters with us.*

Honoring What Was, While Living What Is

Here are some suggested ways you can honor the past while living fully in the present:

Say Their Name

One of the simplest and most powerful ways to honor someone is to say their name out loud. It might feel awkward at first, especially around people who didn't know them, but speaking a loved one's name can keep their presence alive in a gentle, enduring way.

This idea isn't new. Many cultures have, and still do, honor their lost loved ones by saying their names. In ancient Egypt, it was believed a person died twice: once when their body stopped breathing, and again when their name was spoken for the last time. In many African traditions, ancestors are remembered and honored by name during ceremonies and family gatherings. The same practice can be found in many Asian cultures, where the names are spoken out loud or inscribed on tablets. In Japan, it's the Buddhist tradition, the Obon Festival. In China, it's the Qingming Festival (*Tomb Sweeping Day*). In Korean culture, Jesa is an ancestral rite practiced during death anniversaries or holidays. In many Muslim-majority cultures, especially during gatherings after a death, such as the *janāzah* (Islamic funeral prayer and burial service), it is common to say the name of the deceased aloud, share stories about their life, and offer prayers for their soul.

Remembering the dead by name—through spoken prayers, inscriptions, or family rituals—is considered a sacred act of continuity. It reflects not only honor and memory but also the belief that ancestors remain present and influential in family life.

Saying someone's name is a way of saying, *You mattered. You still do.* It doesn't have to be formal. You can speak their name while looking through photos, telling a story, or just remembering something they loved. You can share their name with others who never met them, because part of your legacy may be to carry theirs.

Create a Quiet Ritual

You don't need a public memorial to keep someone close. Small, personal rituals can be just as powerful. As we discussed earlier, you can light a candle or play a song they loved on birthdays or anniversaries. Or keep a framed photo in a meaningful place to keep them present, or cook a favorite meal on a specific date if it brings you comfort.

These are reminders of your loved one, not obligations. Do what feels natural, not forced.

Set Boundaries Around Memories

Some days, memories bring comfort. Other times, they feel like you're drowning, or they're too heavy to bear. When those times come, permit yourself to step in and out of the memories as needed. You might try:

- Keeping a memory box that you can open or close as needed.
- Setting aside a time for looking through photos, rather than getting pulled in every time.
- Deciding which traditions you shared you are going to keep, and which you should adapt or let go of.

Make Space for the Present

There will be times when grief can feel all-consuming, taking up space in our minds, our homes, and even our calendars. But allowing yourself to experience moments of joy doesn't mean you've moved on—it only means you're still moving forward.

Living fully is not a betrayal. It's an act of balance. You're allowed not to wear black. To redecorate. To play music again. To go out to dinner with friends or to throw a party. You're allowed to enjoy yourself without tying every moment of your life to a memory. When you make room for the present, you're not pushing out the past—you're letting both live side by side.

In psychology, the *Dual Process Model of Grief* (Stroebe & Schut)[2] suggests that healthy grieving involves *oscillating*—moving back and forth—between confronting the loss and re-engaging with life. You don't stay in either space permanently. You shift, *loss and life*.

---

[2] Stroebe, Margaret, and Henk Schut. "The Dual Process Model of Coping with Bereavement: Rationale and Description." *Death Studies*, vol. 23, no. 3, 1999, pp. 197-224. Taylor & Francis Online, https://doi.org/10.1080/074811899201046.

Culturally, many traditions make room for laughter and community even during times of mourning. In some African, American, and Caribbean communities, "homegoing" services blend sorrow and celebration. Jewish traditions set specific timeframes for grief, and then it gently nudges mourners back into life. These practices remind us: *It is okay to live.*

The present doesn't have to come at the cost of the past. These simple practices can help you begin living alongside both.

Ways to Reclaim the Present:

- **Redesign your space**

    Rearranging furniture, hanging new art, or adding color can feel like reclaiming part of your environment. This doesn't erase memory—it honors your continued life within it.

- **Start something new**

    Learn a new recipe. Try a new hobby. Join a club or take a class. It doesn't have to be big—it just has to be yours.

- **Mark the calendar with intention**

    Plan small joys: a lunch with a friend, a walk in nature, a movie night. Give yourself things to look forward to—even if you end up changing your mind.

- **Use your hands**

    Writing, gardening, baking, knitting, painting—activities that connect you to the physical world can ground you gently in the here and now.

- **Let light in—literally and emotionally**

    Open a window, uncover a mirror. Play your favorite song. Buy fresh flowers. These aren't frivolous—they're acts of permission.

Try These Gentle Exercises for Reconnecting with Life:

1. **Joy Jar** – Write down one small thing each day that made you smile or feel at peace, and put your note into a jar. On hard days, pull one out and remember it happened.

2. **New Memory Calendar** – Fill a monthly calendar with things you *want* to do—even tiny ones like drinking your favorite tea, taking a walk, or watching a sunset.

3. **Room for Two** – Each week, allow space for both a memory and movement. Visit a grave *and* walk in a new park. Tell a story *and* try a new recipe. You decide.

4. **Music as Mood Medicine** – Create two playlists: one that comforts you in grief and one that lifts your spirits when you're ready. Let them help with whatever you're feeling.

5. **Write a Living Legacy** – Start a memory journal—not just about the person you lost, but about how you're growing. What have they taught you? What values do you want to live by because of them? In doing this, you're letting their story shape the rest of yours.

- Chapter 11 -

Finding New Connections

One of the hardest parts of being the last one standing is the silence...being alone. There's no one left who remembers the stories exactly as you do. No one to say, *"Remember when...?"* and truly mean it. Even joyful old memories can feel oddly flat when there's no longer anyone from your inner circle to share them with.

Grief can isolate anyone, but being the last one standing carries a particular kind of solitude. You may wonder who you are without the roles you used to fill—sibling, child, caretaker, anchor. You may long not just for company, but for that connection that feels meaningful.

The truth is, you still need people. You still need laughter, conversation, and warmth. And even though it may feel different—awkward—or even disloyal, building new connections is a vital part of healing.

Here are some ideas to try:

1. Start Where You Are

You don't have to reinvent your life overnight. Begin by reaching out to someone you already know—an old friend, a neighbor, a cousin you haven't spoken to in a while. A short message, a shared coffee, or even just a check-in phone call can open the door to a new connection. Relationships don't have to be deep right away to be meaningful.

2. Explore New Circles

Consider joining a class, book club, or community group. Volunteering can be especially healing—it gives purpose, structure, and social connection all at once. Become a foster grandmother at a nursery school, or a big sister or brother, or a volunteer in a hospital, nursing home, or for AARP. Many libraries, faith groups, and local nonprofits welcome people who want to give their time, and you might be surprised by who you meet along the way.

3. Share What You're Comfortable Sharing

It can feel strange to talk about your family with people who never knew them, but that doesn't mean you can't. Mentioning your loved ones in conversation doesn't make things awkward; it makes them real. You get to decide what you share and when. Sometimes all it takes is one story to let someone else in.

4. Stay Open to Unexpected Bonds

New relationships may not look anything like the ones you lost. They might come from different generations, backgrounds, or stages of life. That's okay. Don't limit your connections to who "should" understand what you are going through. Sometimes the most healing people are the ones who walk into your life unexpectedly—and stay.

You Still Belong

Grief can make you feel like you're floating along without an anchor. Finding new connections doesn't erase that grief—it simply reminds you that you have the oars to help steer, you're *still a part of something*. Still a part of life. Still connected to the human story, even as the currents in your river shift and change.

You may never again have someone who knows your whole backstory. That can hurt—truly hurt—but it can also free you to create new stories from here, moving forward. You get to be the narrator now, choosing how much of the past to carry forward and how much space to make for moving in the present. As the last one standing, you carry legacy—but you also carry possibility. Finding new connections is one way to keep both alive.

Six Ways to Step Back into Community

Rebuilding connection after a loss can feel daunting, scary, even, but small, intentional steps can open doors to meaningful relationships and renewed purpose. Here are a few steps you can take:

1. **Join a Grief Support Group**

    Connecting with others who understand your experience can provide comfort, validation, clarity, and community. Organizations like *GriefShare* and *Grief in Common* offer both in-person and online support groups tailored to various types of loss.

2. **Join a Grief Book Club**

    Books can help you feel less alone—and reading with others who understand grief can be a quiet but powerful way to reconnect. Groups like the *Faith & Grief Book Club*, *Let's Talk About Loss*, and *Tri-Cities Chaplaincy* offer safe spaces to read, reflect, and share (if you choose). You can also start your own group with help from resources like *Remembering a Life*. Even reading solo—books like *Welcome to the Grief Club* by Janine Kwoh or *The Year of Magical Thinking* by Joan Didion—can be a first step back to community.

3. **Attend Specialized Events**

    Look for events designed to bring people together in remembrance and healing. *The Dinner Party* organizes gatherings for those aged 21-45 who have experienced significant loss, fostering community through shared meals and conversations.

4. **Volunteer Your Time**

    Helping others can be a powerful way to help and heal. Consider volunteering at local community centers, libraries, churches, or organizations that align with your interests. For example, *AARP* offers local volunteer opportunities that address specific community needs, and the Big Brothers Big Sisters matches adult mentors with children and teens to provide guidance, friendship, and support.

5. **Participate in Community Activities**

    Engaging in local events or classes can introduce you to new people and experiences. Libraries, churches, and local schools often host free or low-cost events such as book talks, craft nights, lecture series, or discussion groups. Many churches also offer social gatherings, workshops, or support circles. Whether it's a community supper or an evening class, these events offer easy, low-pressure ways to connect with others while doing something new. Take a look around your own town; your library, recreation center, adult education programs, or nearby church bulletin may hold just the invitation you need.

6. **Explore Online Communities**

    If in-person interactions feel overwhelming for now, online forums and social media groups can provide a sense of connection while maintaining a safe distance. Platforms like *Reddit's Grief Support* offer a place to share experiences anonymously, to ask questions, and find support from others navigating similar journeys.

- Chapter 12 -

Finding Comfort in Being Prepared

Planning ahead isn't always easy—especially when you've already lost so much. The future can feel uncertain, even a little unfair. But taking steps to organize your wishes and documents isn't about giving up; it's about giving yourself (and those who love you) a sense of calm, clarity, and control.

And sometimes, making plans for what's ahead can soften the ache of what's behind you. It gives you something to build, a purpose to seek, and a way to shape meaning from what you've lived through. Planning doesn't erase the pain, but it can ease it. It helps you carry it differently.

When you're the last one standing, your story becomes the thread that ties everything together. If you don't tell it—if you don't write it down—parts of your history may fade with you. Being prepared means more than just legal papers. It also means ensuring that your voice, memories, and legacy aren't lost when you're gone.

This isn't about having all the answers, or even most of them. It's about easing burdens—yours and others'—by making space for comfort, intention, and peace of mind.

Start with the Essentials

It can feel overwhelming to think about your paperwork when your heart is still carrying the loss. But being prepared is an act of care—not just for others, but also for yourself. You've lived through what it feels like when things are left unsaid or undone. Now, you have the chance to shape the way forward with intention and, just maybe, eliminate that undone feeling for your loved ones.

You don't have to do everything all at once. But starting with the basics can lift a quiet weight off your shoulders. Creating or updating simple documents, like a will, an advance healthcare directive, or a list of financial accounts and assets, can help ensure that the people you care about aren't left guessing in a hard moment.

If you're unsure where to start, consider asking your doctor's office or a local hospital for a healthcare directive or proxy form. Many will provide them for free. For a will, some people use a lawyer, while others start with reputable online tools. What matters most is knowing that your wishes are documented in a legally binding way that others can find and follow.

Think of this step not as preparing for the end, but as protecting your peace and giving clarity to those who may one day, in grief, need to act on your behalf.

Where to Keep It

Once you've gathered your important documents, the next step is to ensure they're easily accessible when needed. A will tucked in a drawer or a healthcare directive lost in a stack of papers on your desk won't help anyone take care of you or your wishes in a crisis.

Consider purchasing or creating your own End-of-Life Planner to help organize all your personal information, including medical data, financial records, insurance policies, deeds, and passwords or logins—especially those for your phone and computer. It can also help to include a simple list: who to call and where the rest of your papers can be found. You don't have to make it complicated. You just have to make it clear.

Choose a safe, accessible spot—like a labeled folder in a filing cabinet, a fireproof box, or a secure digital storage service. What matters most is that at least one trusted person will know where it is and how to access it. That might be a family member, a dear friend, or even your attorney or doctor, depending on what's included.

NOTE: When drafting your will, remember, it's about what *you* want done with *your* possessions, money, and property, not what others might think is right or appropriate. You are not obligated to justify your choices or explain your reasoning. And while it may be tempting to share the contents with others ahead of time, be cautious. Revealing too much can stir up emotions, create unrealistic expectations, or even spark conflict. Many relationships have been damaged or destroyed not only by what is or is not in a will, but also by how and when people found out. A well-prepared document, shared at the proper time, can speak for you clearly and kindly, without causing unnecessary pain.

What Do You Want People to Know?

Some things don't belong in a legal document. They belong in your voice, your memories, and your handwritten notes. When you're the last one standing, you carry stories no one else does—stories about the people you've loved, the family you've lost, and the journey you've taken to get here. Don't let those stories vanish!

This is your chance to pass on more than just your things. You can share your values, your lessons, your joys, and your history. You might write letters to your spouse, children, nieces, nephews, godchild, or best friend. You might jot down a favorite recipe, a family saying, or write the story behind an old photo. You could create your own "This is My Story" keepsake journal, telling the journey of your life in your own words and with your own hand. You could even record a short video message, leaving a lasting image of you to help future generations see and hear the person behind the stories.

None of this needs to be polished or perfect. What matters is that it's you, it's real—and that it lasts. These personal touches are often what loved ones remember and treasure most.

Think of it as leaving behind not just instructions, but a connection.

Have That Conversation

Some things are better said than left unsaid. Writing down your wishes is important, but speaking them out loud, when you're ready, can bring clarity and comfort that no document can replace.

You don't need to make a dramatic announcement or cover everything in one sitting. These can be quiet, natural conversations—over coffee, during a walk, over a phone call, or whenever the timing feels right. You might share where your documents are, what matters most to you, that you wish to be cremated, not buried, that you don't want a funeral but a memorial service, or who you'd want to speak for you if you could no longer speak for yourself.

These talks aren't just about logistics. They're about love. You're helping the people around you understand how to honor your life, your choices, and your story. That's a gift.

And if you're not ready to say it yet? Write a note and leave it with your papers. Maybe someday you will choose to have that conversation, or it may just happen spontaneously when the time is right. Whether in person or in writing, the important thing is that your voice will be heard.

- Chapter 13 -

Finding Ways to Prepare for The Next Memory Keeper

"There is an ancient Indian saying that something lives only as long as the last person who remembers it."
Floyd 'Red Crow' Westerman (Dakota Sioux)[3]

Planning ahead isn't just about paperwork and directives, or leaving your personal story. It's also about the memories you carry—the stories, names, and pieces of family history that only you may still know. Just as I've taken steps to prepare for my future, I've come to realize there's another kind of preparation just as important: preserving the past. Because when, like me, you're the last one standing, you're not just the one who makes decisions. You're often the only one who remembers, the torchbearer, the family's memory keeper.

I wish I had opened that photo album my mother kept while she was still here. I wish I had asked her about the faces, the names, the moments caught in those pages. Maybe then, I would know those stories, and I could pass them along with the photos. Maybe my sister and I wouldn't have had to guess who they were after Mom died. And maybe, just maybe, those people could still be remembered. It's important to me, especially now, to keep our cherished memories alive.

---

[3] Floyd 'Red Crow' Westerman (Dakota Sioux), Facebook, February 17, 2024.

I understand I won't always be here to carry the torch. That's a quiet truth I've come to accept. Because of this, I've started thinking about how to make room for whoever may come after me. I don't yet know who that person will be—a niece, a nephew, a grandchild (I wish), or a younger cousin not yet born. But I want them to have something to hold onto, something to pass along. I want to leave behind more than just names and dates on our family tree in Ancestry.com. I want to leave the family stories, the meaning, and the love.

So, as the memory keepers, *we* have to begin to prepare for those who follow as the Keepers.

Preparing the Ground

This isn't about getting everything in perfect order. It's more about leaving a trail—something the next memory keeper can follow when it's their turn.

A. Organize What You Can Gather

Start looking through what you already have:

- **Photos** — Take the time to label some, even if it's just a guess. Who's in the picture, where it might have been taken, and what you remember about that day.

- **Documents** — Old letters, birth certificates, marriage licenses, diplomas, obituaries, church programs. Tuck them into folders or envelopes, so they stay together.

- **Keepsakes** — There are probably more than a few small things that hold big meaning—a recipe card, an apron, a piece of jewelry, a watch or bracelet, a Sunday hat. Jot down a note or two about what they are, who they belonged to, and why they matter.

Even when you don't remember all the details, write what you can. "Uncle John, maybe taken at Aunt Jane's house, sometime in the '80s." That's enough. It's a thread someone else can pull.

B. Write Down What Only You Know

There are things only you remember—and if you don't write them down, they could disappear. Little things. A favorite song. A family nickname. A family trip. The way mother used to hum while cooking. The goofy way father laughed. Stop waiting for the perfect moment to write them all down. Just begin. You can scribble a few lines in a notebook or type a memory on your computer. If you don't feel like writing, you can speak into your cellphone's recorder. It doesn't have to be fancy. It just has to be real.

Here are a few prompts that may help open the door:

- "One thing I never want forgotten is…"
- "Here's how I remember Grandma's kitchen…"
- "Mom's favorite song was…"
- "Dad's favorite food was…"
- "The first family trip that I remember was to…"
- "This is the story behind that photo of Uncle Joe in the blue car…"

Even a few words can carry a lifetime's worth of meaning.

Making It Easy to Find

You can begin by sorting things into simple folders—some can be physical, and some digital, if that's your way. You can save copies of photos, scan papers, and write brief notes to explain what's maintained and where. You don't need to create a museum to leave behind a map.

This is for the next storyteller, your family memory keeper— but it's also for anyone who may one day wonder, *Where do I come from? Who were the people who made me who I am? What were they like?*

When they go looking, hopefully, they will find something waiting for them. Something they can pass on.

- Chapter 14 -

Conclusion

Finding Joy Without Guilt

Grief is different for everyone. But one thing is the same—grief does not disappear all at once. It walks beside you—sometimes quietly, sometimes with a heavy step. For some, the walk is long; for others, it softens sooner—but it is always a journey. As the road stretches out ahead of you, there will come a moment when the clouds shift, just slightly, and the sun breaks through. You may catch yourself laughing. You may be enjoying a quiet afternoon. And then, just as suddenly, you feel it: guilt.

It's a familiar, quiet ache—the sense that if you're still moving forward, you must be leaving someone behind. That if you laugh, you're forgetting. That if you feel joy, you're somehow dishonoring the loss you still carry.

But here's the truth: joy does not erase grief. It walks alongside it. It means that your heart, even after being broken, can still mend. That the love and grief you've carried haven't stopped you—they've simply changed the way you walk now.

There's no map for finding when joy will return. You don't have to chase it or explain it, and you can't push it. But when it does show up—like a sunny afternoon after a cloudy morning—let it walk with you. Let it warm your face, lighten your step, and lift your spirits. Joy doesn't mean you've moved on. It means you're moving *with*.

You're not leaving your loved one behind on this road. You're carrying them with you—step by step—into new places, new moments, and new memories they helped make possible. And there is no greater act of remembrance than that.

> *"And as each day goes by,*
> *I get a little bit stronger*
> *But that don't stop me from wishing you were here*
> *a little bit longer."*
> William Dempsey, From *Beat You There*

Still Walking...Forward

You've made it through pages that weren't easy. Some of them asked you to remember. Others asked you to imagine what comes next. And through it all, you've kept walking.

Being the last one standing doesn't mean standing still. It means standing with memory. Standing with love. Standing with the weight of what was, and the courage to keep going anyway.

Along this path, you may still trip over sadness or get caught in the tangle of unanswered questions. That's okay. Keep walking because there will also be times when light filters through the trees, casting sun on your face, and the path is free of stones. There will also be unexpected laughter and moments that feel like grace on your journey.

If this book has done anything, let it be this: a hand on your shoulder. A quiet companion. A gentle hug. Mostly, a reminder that you are not alone—not in your grief, not in your healing, not as the memory keeper, and not in your hope.

CONCLUSION

You're still walking forward. Step by step, story by story, day by day. And, for now, let that be enough.

Acknowledgements

Writing this book has been both the hardest and most healing thing I've ever written. Grief has walked beside me for so much of my life, showing up in different forms and at different times over the years. But losing my sister—the one who shared my history, my heart, and so many of my days—brought a grief I didn't know how to carry. She was my better, happier half, the keeper of memories I hadn't even remembered forgetting.

Writing about the losses I've experienced, and especially this last one, helped me find a clearer way forward. In putting words to my sorrow, I've seen moments of light. In facing the emptiness, I've uncovered quiet spaces of strength within myself. This book didn't take the pain away, but it helped me make room for it—and, somehow, make peace with what remains.

To my sister Janyra, my "J", there are no words big enough or deep enough to hold what you meant to me. You were my partner in childhood mischief, anchor in my storms, co-keeper of memories, and the one person who knew the unspoken things. We finished each other's thoughts, sentences, and champagne. Where I was the serious one, you were the silly one—always ready with a grin, or a look that said, "Lighten up, it'll be okay." We didn't just grow up together—we grew *through* life together.

Losing you broke something open in me, leaving some place raw and painful. But writing this has been a way to sit with you again, to remember not just how you left but how you *lived*. Your laugh still echoes. Your stories still shine. Your smile still warms. Your love still holds. I carry it all forward in my head and heart—with gratitude, with ache, with every word written here.

To my husband, "B", thank you for being my rock through it all. Through the long months of caring for my sister, the constant interruptions to our lives and plans, the last-minute plane trips, the hospital and hospice visits, the packing and moving of her things, you showed up, again and again. You held me together when I felt like I was falling apart. Then, and still now. And while you carried so much of my grief, you were carrying your own too, because she was like a sister to you, not just in name but in heart. Your love, your patience, your quiet strength gave me the space to grieve, to remember, and eventually, to write. I couldn't have done this without you.

To my dear friend, Christine, thank you for going out of your way to travel to be with J when she was sick. For looking out for her, taking her to doctor's appointments, picking up her groceries or medications, and simply sitting with her. You gave her comfort and gave me peace of mind from afar. I am forever grateful for the care and compassion you showed her. And most of all, thank you for driving up to be with me the day after she died. Your love, your warmth, your friendship—just your *presence*—carried me through one of the hardest days of my life. I don't know how I would have gotten through it without you.

To my two children, Sha and "E", thank you for your love and support throughout this long and winding journey of grief. And to my daughter especially, thank you for being there when it mattered most. You sat by my sister's side as she left this world, offering comfort, calm, and love when I wasn't able to be there myself. I will always be grateful for your gift of presence and love to her.

To my editor, Shamila Iyer—you were the first and only person to read my full manuscript, whose concept I had only recently shared with my husband. That alone was a leap of faith. Your kind words after reading it brought me to tears. This book was never easy to write, but your encouragement gave me the confidence to keep going. Thank you for meeting my story with such compassion and care. Your insight, assistance, knowledge, and steady guidance helped me shape something so personal into something I could finally let go of. This is my first book—and likely will be my most emotional—and I'm so grateful you were the one to help carry it forward.

And to you, dear reader, thank you. Whether you are in the thick of grief, quietly carrying your losses, or slowly learning how to live as the last one standing or the memory keeper, you are not alone. And if you are someone trying to help, support, or understand a person walking through this journey of grief, I hope these pages offered some insight, some language, or even just a little light so you may understand or support someone suffering the loss of a loved one. This book was written from the tenderest place in my heart, and if even one sentence gave you comfort, clarity, the courage to keep going on your journey, or to support another on their journey, then it has done what I hoped it would. Grief changes us. But so does love. And memory, when spoken and shared, keeps what matters alive. I'm honored you have chosen to walk a little of your journey alongside mine.

Appendix

The following are a few of the many organizations that offer grief-related education, counseling, conversation, and community resources. These tools may be beneficial for individuals navigating personal loss, grieving, mourning, and emotional healing.

Alliance of Hope for Suicide Loss Survivors – They provide healing and compassionate support in a 24/7 forum to help people survive suicide loss. https://allianceofhope.org

Cruse Bereavement Care – This UK-based organization offers free counseling, information, and opportunities for bereaved individuals to connect through in-person, online, or in support groups. https://www.cruse.org.uk

Good Mourning – An Australian-based podcast and grief support community offering candid conversations, live events, workshops, expert interviews, and practical tools for navigating grief. https://www.goodmourning.com.au

Grief Recovery After Substance Passing. GRASP – Provides support groups that offer comfort and healing for families or individuals in the United States and Canada who have lost someone to drug use or addiction. https://grasphelp.org

Grief in Common – Offers day and evening online live chat rooms & individual grief coaching for every type of loss. https://www.griefincommon.com

GriefShare – Offers free faith-based 13-week in-person or online grief recovery support groups. https://www.griefshare.org

Hospice Foundation of America – Provides resources to families and individuals for hospice and End-of-Life care, and bereavement and grief support. https://hospicefoundation.org

National Alliance for Children's Grief – Lists grief support service providers, and provides education and support for grieving children and teens. https://childrengrieve.org

Psychology Today Therapist Finder – Search by location, insurance, specialty, or by gender, race, religion, or identity to find a licensed therapist. https://psychologytoday.com/us/therapists

Reddit – r/GriefSupport – Provides a moderated online community where people can share personal experiences, ask questions, and give and receive advice and support related to grief and loss. The site offers peer encouragement, coping strategies, and a sense of connection for those navigating bereavement. www.reddit.com/r/GriefSupport

The Compassionate Friends – With more than 500 chapters across the United States, TCF provides personal comfort and support to families who have lost a son or a daughter, a brother or a sister, or a grandchild, as well as help so others can better assist the grieving family. https://www.compassionatefriends.org

The Dinner Party – Connects young adult grievers aged 21- 45 to a caring and supportive in-person or virtual community of peer grievers who help each other navigate loss, life, and grief. https://www.thedinnerparty.org

The Dougy Center – Offers resources and no-cost peer support groups nationally and internationally for grieving children, teens, and families. It provides a place for individuals to go to seek help both before and after a death. https://www.dougy.org

The Sibling Grief Club – An online resource and supportive community for adults who are grieving the loss of a sibling. They offer webinars, self-care tips, articles, a Facebook support group, and helpful tools tailored to sibling grief. https://siblinggriefclub.com

Therapy for Black Girls – Offers a therapist directory, mental health and wellness support, and a podcast "Healing in Real Time", for girls and women of color. https://www.therapyforblackgirls.com

What's Your Grief – Provides grief support and guidance with resources, including online courses, podcasts, and articles for those suffering from grief, and education and training for grief counselors. https://whatsyourgrief.com

Bibliography

Adam Koenig, M.A. *The Healing Power of Grief Rituals. Grief Rituals: Definition, Examples, & Ideas to Try.* Choosing Therapy. March 29, 2023. https://www.choosingtherapy.com/grief-rituals

Alan D. Wolfelt, Ph.D. *Helping Yourself Heal When an Adult Sibling Dies.* Center for Loss. December 21, 2023. https://www.centerforloss.com/2023/12/helping-heal-adult-sibling-dies/

American Heart Association. *Día de los Muertos Celebrates the Life of the Deceased.* AHA News. October 31, 2023. https://www.heart.org/en/news/2023/10/31/dia-de-los-muertos-celebrates-the-life-of-the-deceased-while-easing-the-grief-of-the-living

Audrey Glickman. *Why Do We Say "May Her Memory Be for a Blessing"?* Congregation Beth Shalom. September 25, 2020. https://bethshalompgh.org/why-do-we-say-may-her-memory-be-for-a-blessing

Avidan Milevsky Ph.D. *When a Sibling Dies: The plight of siblings who have lost a major part of their life.* Psychology Today. August 2, 2020. https://www.psychologytoday.com/us/blog/band-brothers-and-sisters/202008/when-sibling-dies

Bible. Proverbs 10:7 – *The memory of the righteous is for a blessing…* BibleHub.com, n.d. https://biblehub.com/proverbs/10-7.htm

Chickasaw Nation. *Keepers of the Flame.* Chickasaw Cultural Center. n.d. https://www.chickasaw.net/Our-Nation/Culture/Arts/Storytellers.aspx, ADA News. December 19, 2024. https://www.theadanews.com/news/local_news/keepers-of-the-flame-storytellers-charged-with-sustaining-chickasaw-essence/article_4cd88424-bd88-11ef-a057-13fc9778e9ee.html

David B. Feldman, Ph.D. *The Power of Rituals to Heal Grief.* Psychology Today. September 28, 2019. https://www.psychologytoday.com/us/blog/supersurvivors/201909/the-power-rituals-heal-grief

Donna Ashworth. *I Am the Taker of the Photos.* From the book *'Growing Brave'*, Black & White Publishing, 2024. https://www.facebook.com/donnaashworthwords/posts/i-am-the-taker-of-the-photosi-am-the-receiver-of-the-groans-they-eye-rolls-and-t/1030077178481011/

Edward Hirsch. From *Gabriel: A Poem.* Knopf. 2014. https://edwardhirsch.com/gabriel-a-poem-2/

Elisabeth Kübler-Ross. *On Death and Dying.* Scribner. 1969.

Emily Dickinson. *Unable are the Loved to die.* From the book *The Complete Poems of Emily Dickinson*, Little, Brown. Jan.1960. p.809, originally published 1890

Floyd "Red Crow" Westerman. Facebook. February 17, 2024

Harvard Health Publishing. *Writing to Ease Grief and Loss.* Harvard Health Blog. Nov. 15, 2016. https://www.health.harvard.edu/mind-and-mood/writing-to-ease-grief

Hospice Foundation of America. *Grief and Self-Care.* Hospice Foundation of America, n.d. https://hospicefoundation.org/Grief-(1)/Grief-and-Self-Care

Ian Reader. *Religion in Contemporary Japan.* Honolulu: University of Hawai'i Press. 1991. https://archive.org/details/religionincontem0000read/page/10/mode/

Idara Al Furqan. *What is Janazah? All You Need To Know.* November 23, 2023. https://idaraalfurqan.com/what-is-janazah-all-you-need-to-know/

Janine Kwoh. *Welcome to the Grief Club: Because You Don't Have to Go Through It Alone.* Workman Publishing Company, 2022.

Jo Christner, Psy.D. *Finding Balance in Your Grieving.* HOPE Connection. June 18, 2022. https://hopegroups.org/finding-balance-in-your-grieving%EF%BF%BC/

Joan Didion. *The Year of Magical Thinking.* Knopf, 2005.

Jodi Picoult. *My Sister's Keeper.* Turtleback Books. 2005

Kahlil Gibran. *On Joy and Sorrow.* From "*The Prophet.*" United States. A. A. Knopf, 1923.

Kami Fletcher, Ph.D. *7 Elements of African American Mourning Practices & Burial Traditions.* TalkDeath.com. February 8, 2021. https://talkdeath.com/7-elements-of-african-american-mourning-practices-burial-traditions

Keanu Reeves. "*I don't want to flee from Life*". By Dotson Rader. The Modesto Bee. June 11, 2006. pp.100-101. https://www.newspapers.com/image/698247279/?clipping_id=110644194

Kenneth J. Doka, Ph.D. *When Siblings Grieve: The importance of support for adults grieving the loss of a sibling.* Psychology Today. February 23, 2025. https://www.psychologytoday.com/us/blog/good-mourning/202501/when-siblings-grieve

Laurel J. Kiser, et al. *Who Are We, But for the Stories We Tell: Family Stories and Healing.* Psychol Trauma: NIH Public Access. September 1, 2010. pp 243-249
https://www.ncbi.nlm.nih.gov/pmc/articles/PMC3010736/

Lili'uokalani Trust. *Kaumaha Helu 'Ekahi: Traditional Hawaiian Beliefs about Dying, Death and 'Uhane*. Onipaa.org, n.d. https://onipaa.org/kaumaha-helu-ekahi

Margaret Stroebe & Henk Schut. *The Dual Process Model of Coping with Bereavement*. Death Studies. 1999. https://doi.org/10.1080/074811899201046

Maria Lynders. *Indigenous Storytellers Work to Protect and Pass Down Tribal Knowledge to Next Generation*. WSHU / Connecticut News, November 15, 2023. https://www.wshu.org/connecticut-news/2023-11-15/ct-indigenous-storytellers-pass-down-tribal-knowledge

Marilyn A. Mendoza, Ph.D. *How Journaling Can Help You Grieve*. Psychology Today. January 26, 2021. https://www.psychologytoday.com/us/blog/understanding-grief/202101/how-journaling-can-help-you-grieve

National Cancer Institute. *Grief, Bereavement, and Loss*. National Cancer Institute. Updated February 12, 2025. https://www.cancer.gov/about-cancer/advanced-cancer/caregivers/planning/bereavement-pdq

National Institute on Aging. *Coping with Grief and Loss*. U.S. Department of Health & Human Services, 2022. https://www.nia.nih.gov/health/grief-and-mourning/coping-grief-and-loss

Sarah L. Delany and A. Elizabeth Delany. *Having Our Say: The Delany Sisters' First 100 Years*. Kodansha America. 1993.

William Dempsey. From *Beat You There*. Lyrics by Will Dempsey. January 2022.

Yumi Sakugawa. From *There Is No Right Way to Meditate: And Other Lessons*. Adams Media. 2015.

About The Author

P. J. Johnson is a retired employment and civil rights trial attorney who stopped writing and arguing legal briefs when COVID-19 upended the world. She also served as an administrative law judge for both the Human Rights Division and the Health Department, and worked as an arbitrator in small claims court. Paula is married and the mother of two grown children—a daughter and a son—both of whom are independent and making their own way in the world. But titles aside, according to Paula, the most defining role she's had more recently is that of memory keeper—the last one standing in her immediate family. She spends part of her time searching, capturing, setting down, and preserving her family history—names, stories, photographs, and moments—for the generations that will come after her. Paula says, "It's my way of making sure we are not forgotten."

These days, Paula enjoys traveling with her husband—her best friend for over 35 years, aside from her sister—and trying to keep her sister's joyful outlook on life alive, even amid the heaviness now surrounding us in the world. She has also returned to something she long put off: writing. Paula has begun a series on women pioneers and is also finishing a children's book. Now that she has retired, she finally has the time to write, bake, garden, and even grow some of her own food.

And when the weight of it all feels like too much, Paula goes to her comfort spot: the beach. That's why she has always lived close to the ocean. "Sitting quietly, listening to the waves, letting them carry my thoughts in and out with the tide—that's where I breathe, where I feel closest to peace, and where I remember how to begin again."

Your Feedback Matters!

Your thoughts mean the world to me. Reviews not only help me grow as an author—they also help other readers discover books that may support them on their journey.

If this book spoke to you in any way, I'd be so grateful if you could take a moment to share your honest review on Amazon. It doesn't have to be long—just a few words about what stood out to you or how it helped. Simply scan the QR code using the camera on your smartphone. Then, tap the notification that appears on your phone, and it will direct you to the page to leave a review.

Thank you for reading, for sharing, and for being part of this community of hope and healing.

My Gift to You

In case you don't already have a notepad set aside for jotting down your thoughts, feelings, or responses, or if you'd like one that follows along with *Last One Standing*, I've created a companion workbook. It includes the same reflections, prompts, and "Try This" exercises from this book, along with extra space for your journaling. This workbook is simply another tool designed to help you capture your responses and reflect more deeply on your feelings as you navigate your journey at your own pace. For you, my fellow traveler, it's free as a *thank you* for purchasing my book.

To receive your free copy, just email me at **contact@michevanpublishing.com** with the subject line "**Workbook**," and I'll send it to you with my thanks.

www.ingramcontent.com/pod-product-compliance
Lightning Source LLC
Chambersburg PA
CBHW071403130526
44581CB00015B/133/J